First edition published in the United States of America by
the Global Association of Risk Professionals

111 Town Square Place, Suite 1215
Jersey City, NJ, 07310, U.S.A.
Tel: +1 201.719.7210 • Fax: +1 201.222.5022

2nd Floor, Bengal Wing, 9A Devonshire Square
London, EC2M 4YN, U.K.
Tel: + 44 (0) 20 7397 9630 • Fax: +44 (0) 20 7626 9300
Website: www.garp.org

ISBN: 978-1-933861-02-9
Printed in the United States of America

Table of Contents

Introduction

The global financial crisis accentuated the responsibility of financial institutions to manage their risks. In the wake of the spectacular, unprecedented and fundamental transformation of the global financial infrastructure, the responsibility of risk managers has changed. At financial institutions worldwide, banks and regulators increasingly rely on the skills, knowledge and integrity of risk managers to pilot the transformation of the financial system as it becomes more risk aware with improved risk management policies, practices, and systems.

As risk management has moved to the forefront of banking, risk managers are becoming more and more visible, important and trusted at banks. This evolution is driven both by the banks themselves and by supervisors: banks are increasingly sensitive to the materiality of risks in their decision making policies, and supervisors, all around the world, have come to recognize that better understanding of risk management principles and practices is vital, not only for the success of individual banks, but also for the safety and soundness of the global financial infrastructure.

As a result, leading banking supervisors from all around the world have further refined those regulations that were outlined by the Basel Committee on Banking Supervision in the *International Convergence of Capital Measurement and Capital Standards*, also known as the Basel II Accord. These new changes and proposals reflect the new financial world order and codify experiences of the risk management practices of many highly regarded banks. While this present book does not specifically address the Basel II Accord and its ongoing enhancements, conceptually it owes a great deal to the principles and practices embraced by the Accord. These principles and practices integrate qualitative and quantitative components.

Integrated Bank Risk Management is part of the *GARP Risk Series* that offers a qualitative introduction to banking risks, bank risk management, and the international risk-based regulation of banks. The goal of *Integrated Bank Risk Management* and other related volumes in this series is to ensure that the reader develops a deep understanding of the qualitative aspects of a typical, large bank's risk management activities, including risk assessment, measurement, modeling and management, across the trading and banking books. This book focuses on contemporary risk methodologies covering the interest rate risk in the banking book, liquidity risk, and capital management and risk management practices at banks and financial institutions.

All a part of the *GARP Risk Series, Market Risk Management, Credit Risk Management, Operational Risk Management* and *Integrated Bank Risk Management* enhance the understanding of specific risks and emphasize the right questions to ask when qualitatively analyzing the risks of various financial instruments or assets.

These books create a broad based understanding of the chief risks banks face and how these risks can be best managed. Understanding the specific sources of risks is essential in the management process of measuring, monitoring, and managing risk. The material is presented in a user-friendly format enabling readers to understand the key qualitative risk factors and how they drive bank risk management. Each book contains numerous examples of actual financial events, as well as case studies, diagrams, and tables aimed at explaining these complex relationships. Overall, these volumes foster a better understanding of why and how financial risks emerge and how these risks can impact individual financial assets, financial institutions, financial systems, and ultimately, the global financial infrastructure.

Students who successfully complete market, credit, operational and integrated risk management readings will gain a broad understanding of how the various risks reinforce each other, and are strongly encouraged to sit for GARP's *International Certificate in Banking Risk and Regulation*, an integrated look at the chief risks financial institutions face and how to best manage them. To complete the program, students will be required to review and understand certain assigned additional readings, and to take and pass a certification exam.

These readings contain several technical terms used in banking and risk management. While the material requires a fundamental understanding of finance and banking, the intended readers are not practicing risk managers but bankers who want to have a better understanding of the qualitative factors affecting risks and who have familiarity with fundamental banking and finance concepts. This study text has adopted the standard codes used by banks throughout the world to identify currencies for the purposes of trading, settlement and the displaying of market prices. The codes, set by the International Organization for Standardization (ISO), avoid the confusion that could result as many currencies have similar names. For example, the text uses USD for the U.S. dollar, GBP for the British pound, EUR for the euro, and JPY for the Japanese yen.

Acknowledgements

Integrated Risk Management, a part of the *GARP Risk Series*, has been developed under the auspices of the Banking Risk and Regulation Committee at GARP who guided and reviewed the work of the contributing authors. The Committee, chaired by Professor Xavier Freixas, dean of the undergraduate School of Economics and Business Administration and professor at the Universitat Pompeu Fabra in Barcelona (Spain) and Research Fellow at CEPR, oversaw the strategic development of the program.

The committee and the authors thank Dr. Viktor Makarov, Head of Quantitative Analytics at MetLife and member of GARP's Board of Trustees, Dr. Benton E. Gup, professor of Finance at the University of Alabama, and Dr. Christopher Donohue, Managing Director of the GARP Research Center, who contributed to the development of the program.

Last, but not least, the authors thank Mr. Richard Apostolik, the President and CEO of GARP, who has recognized the importance practice-driven risk education plays in strengthening the future resiliency of the global financial system, and is a tireless champion of risk management, risk managers and risk education. Without his vigorous advocacy for risk management and risk managers, education benefitting the global financial system would not have been made possible.

Introduction to Integrated Bank Risk Management

Integrated Bank Risk Management, a volume in the *GARP Risk Series*, focuses on integrated risk management by analyzing how risk drives capital management decisions for banks. It consists of three chapters: the first focuses on the interest rate risk in the banking book, the second focuses on liquidity risk, and the third focuses on capital management. In analyzing the interest rate risk in the banking book, the readings focus on the role a bank's treasury function plays in managing the comprehensive risk exposures of the bank, including the measurement and management of asset and liability exposures, and various alternative approaches to better understand these. In analyzing the liquidity risk, the readings focus on the various types of liquidity, sources of liquidity problems, and the potential costs of mismanaging liquidity risk. In analyzing capital management in banks, the readings focus on the types and roles of capital, and how risk adjusted capital has evolved as an important tool to manage banks. Thus, this capstone volume focuses on the economics of risk management and not on the regulation of risk management.

Chapter 1

Interest Rate Risk in the Banking Book

In this chapter, we focus on how banks manage the interest rate risk in their banking book, i.e. the risk related to non-traded assets and liabilities such as loans and deposits. The interest rate risk in the banking book differs from credit or default risk: it relates to the impact interest rate changes may have on the value of the loans and deposits, and by extension, the overall earnings and the value of the bank.

We begin with an overview of asset and liability management (ALM), which includes interest rate risk in the banking book and liquidity risk management, the latter of which is covered in Chapter 2. Bank capital management is also sometimes considered part of treasury risk, but it can also fall in the strategic planning area. This topic is discussed in detail in Chapter 3.

On completion of this chapter the reader will have a basic understanding of:

- The role of the treasury function in different types of banks
- Types of treasury risk
- The importance of asset and liability management (ALM) in banks
- The objectives of an ALM program
- The nature of interest rate risk in the banking book: net interest income and bank equity
- How interest rate risk is measured and managed in the banking book
- Strengths and weaknesses of models used to manage ALM market risk

1.1 THE ROLE OF THE TREASURY

The Treasury function plays a significant role in managing a bank's assets and liabilities, its liquidity and its capital. The Treasury can also play many different roles in a bank; the exact roles vary significantly depending on the business model adopted by the bank.

Most treasury functions take an active role in managing the bank's balance sheet capital — the debt and equity the bank has raised to finance its assets. Capital can either be equity capital or debt, and thus has multiple meanings. For instance, accounting equity capital is the equity capital the bank has raised from shareholders and from its earnings. Typically, equity capital satisfies regulatory capital, but there may be other types of capital than equity capital that are eligible to meet regulatory capital requirements. Additionally, the financing sources may also include debt, both long-term borrowings and deposits.

Some capital requires no interest payments (such as equity and reserves), but most capital comes in the form of interest-bearing deposits, interbank loans and securities. The collective capital is invested to generate a cash return, the risk of which depends on how the capital is allocated to different types of interest-bearing assets. This gives the bank an interest "net position" (it earns interest on the assets and pays interest on the funding) that must be managed to avoid volatile profit and losses as interest rates move This is one type of interest rate risk the bank bears. Fluctuations in interest rates also create "equity risk" for the bank as the value of its assets and liabilities change.

While the bank treasury performs standard corporate treasury functions, such as security issuance, cash forecasting and management, financial decision-making and insurance, for example, the role of the Treasury in a bank is greater because of the large number of financial functions in the bank. While every bank has slightly different functions, a large number fit into one of two models: a commercial/retail model, or a commercial/retail with investment banking model. The typical function of the treasury in these two bank types is described below.

1.1.1 A Commercial/Retail Only Bank Model

A typical commercial/retail bank model focuses its asset strategy on commercial and retail loans, and funds the loans using a combination of equity, retained earnings, deposits, publicly issued bonds and interbank loans. It may seem that a bank of this type would focus on its underwriting risk, and as long there were not too many commercial or retail defaults, the bank would perform well. This simplification is incorrect. It is possible that the bank could have an extremely good underwriting department but could still lose a great deal of money due to fluctuations in interest rates. Interest rates could affect its income adversely and could also affect its balance sheet adversely.

As an example of income effects, suppose the bank had entered into a number of long-term commercial and retail loans at fixed rates prevailing at the time the loans were originated. If interest rates subsequently rose, the bank would have to pay higher interest rates to its depositors and would have to pay higher rates on its debt to the extent the debt interest rate was linked to floating indices, or to the extent the debt used to fund the loans was of a shorter maturity than the loans. If rates rose, a bank could actually end up in a negative cash flow position even in the absence of defaults.

As an example of balance sheet effect, if rates rose, the same bank would see its fixed rate assets drop in value, although that effect would be offset by a reduction in the value of its fixed rate liabilities. Floating rate assets and liabilities would not change much in value. This affects the value of the equity of the bank, since equity is the difference between assets and liabilities. For that reason, this risk is sometimes called equity risk. If fixed rate assets dominated fixed rate liabilities, as would be the case for most commercial/retail banks, rising interest rates would damage the bank's equity value.

Treasuries in commercial/retail banks are likely to manage the net interest rate risk in their banking book directly with market counterparties by operating a derivatives trading desk. In the bank described above, to protect against rising interest rates, the bank would enter interest rate swaps where it paid fixed rates and received floating rates to offset the risk of its fixed rate assets (see Chapter 3). The objective, as explained later in this section, is to manage the interest margin of the bank: the return the bank earns on its assets such as loans and investments, and the funding cost of these, such as the interest paid on deposits.

International commercial/retail banks have foreign exchange risk in their operations due to foreign operating expenses such as salaries and property leases. In these cases, the management of the attendant foreign exchange exposure will often fall to the treasury as well.

Some banks treat their treasury unit as a cost center that primarily focuses on managing interest rate and foreign exchange risk. Others run their Treasury function as a profit-making business unit. This particularly holds true in developed markets, while in emerging and developing markets, the Treasury supports the overall activities of the bank. Larger banks in the emerging and developing markets may task their Treasury function with managing their foreign currency exposure.

For instance, if a bank has substantial commercial and retail business, and the currency in which it primarily operates is not a major currency, then the Treasury may manage the interest rate risk positions for profit. The constant business coming from the lending and deposit gathering of the bank's commercial and retail business results in its being well positioned to exploit its commercial position in domestic currency interest rate risk markets. When the same commercial position results in the bank executing significant orders from its customers for foreign currency transactions, the Treasury may in fact run complex trading operations.

Banks may operate in a heavily traded currency where there are substantial institutional counterparties, including investment banks and hedge funds. In this situation it is likely that a commercial and retail bank's treasury operations will primarily be focused on ensuring that the risks generated by the bank's businesses are covered in the market. Such treasury operations are commonly known as cover operations. They make sure that the profits generated by the customer business are not damaged by the failure to manage the inherent market risk, e.g. the interest rate or foreign exchange risk in the banking book.

1.1.2 A Commercial/Retail Bank with an Investment Banking Operation Business Model

For banks with an investment banking operation actively engaged in traded market risk and managing it for profit, the Treasury function is likely to be primarily concerned with the effective transfer of interest rate risk in the banking book to the investment bank at a fair transfer price. Here a central Treasury function serves other parts of the bank and provides a support function to those commercial and investment banking operations that are more directly client focused.

The central Treasury may be responsible for managing the retail market risk function of a commercial/retail bank with an investment banking operation. However, some banks with investment banking operations permit their commercial and retail businesses to manage their individual banking book risks directly with the investment banking operation. In this business model the Treasury takes on the role of monitoring and regulating the management of interest rate risk in the banking book, while retaining its group-wide liquidity and capital management activities.

Ensuring the smooth flow of such business will require 'running'/taking on trading positions to manage these risks. However, such risks are likely to be of a limited nature.

In general terms, this is the model followed by JPMChase, as described in their 2007 Annual Report. Most other banks that do not have the same size and strategic breadth as JPMChase tend to follow the first approach — the commercial/retail banking approach.

1.2 TREASURY RISK

Treasury risk is defined as the risk of loss in the activities of a bank's Treasury. It is also sometimes used to mean ALM risk alone. Since every Treasury operates slightly differently, however, the term "Treasury risk" can be ambiguous. Here is one example of an integrated bank treasury function:

Figure 1: Treasury Risk

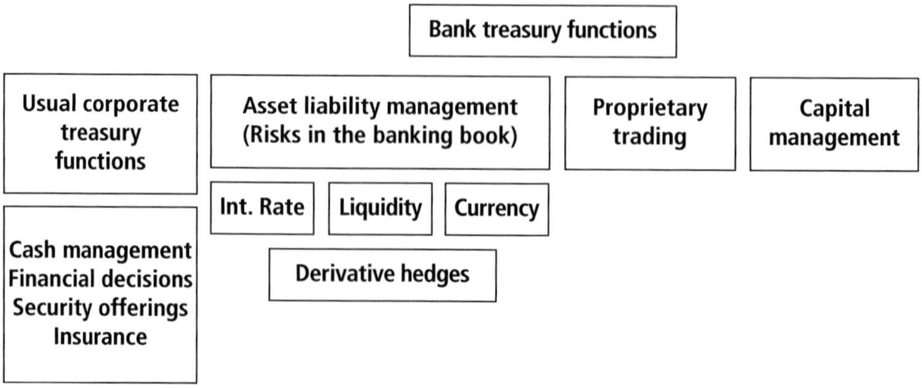

In this text we focus only on:

- Interest rate risk in the banking book (this chapter)
- Liquidity risk, or the management of the balance sheet and its funding (Chapter 2)
- Proprietary trading (Chapter 2)
- Capital management (Chapter 3)

To avoid confusion in the rest of this volume, we will refer to specific treasury functions where applicable and avoid the generalized term "Treasury risk."

1.3 ASSET AND LIABILITY MANAGEMENT ACTIVITIES

While the treasury usually manages ALM risk, it often does so under the oversight of an Asset Liability Committee (ALCO) or in some cases the Risk Management Committee. The role of the traditional ALCO is defined by the American Banker:[1]

> *"A committee, usually comprising senior managers, responsible for managing assets and liabilities to maximize income and safety over the long run. In a financial institution, the ALCO is usually responsible for asset and liability distribution, asset and liability pricing, balance sheet size, funding, spread management, and interest rate sensitivity management."*

In most banks asset and liability management has the primary objective of managing the impact of interest rate risk in the bank's balance sheet and ensuring that the interest rate risk inherent in the bank's underlying business does not disrupt the production of a stable income stream over time.

Asset and liability management is not just concerned with managing risk and stabilizing business value. It is also concerned with:

- Maintaining the desired liquidity structure of a bank as seen in the next chapter
- Other factors affecting the structure and composition of a bank's balance sheet
- Circumstances impacting the stability of income the bank generates over time

There are numerous problems due to the need to balance the structure and composition of a bank's balance sheet. Many of these are related to the problems international banks face as they have capital structures dominated by their home currency, but whose earnings and many of their assets and liabilities are in other currencies. This introduces foreign exchange risk (see Chapter 2) into the bank's earnings. For example, the present and future profits from overseas operations may be volatile when translated into the bank's domestic currency due to changes in the exchange rate, which are affected by differences in interest rates. Similarly, domestic currency denominated capital that has been allocated to overseas operations supports an asset structure denominated in a different, foreign, currency. Since exchange rates and profitability can change, the dual effect of these changes introduce volatility into the capital requirements and may reduce the ability to meet regulatory minimum standards.

Asset and liability management is often described as using risk management techniques employed by bond portfolio managers and applying them to the repricing of interest rates on retail assets and liabilities (see Chapter 3). The reason is that the cash flows investments and loans the bank holds on its balance sheet and deposits that the bank finances these assets with can be modeled as cash flows generated by bonds. While in many ways this is true, the asset and liability manager has to recognize the following:

- A bank's balance sheet is a dynamic collection of assets and liabilities because new loans and deposits are continuously being made and others mature.
- Repricing of the assets and liabilities on a bank's balance sheet is not all contractual since often there are significant timing differences between changes in market rates affecting the pricing of wholesale credit and deposit products and changes in the interest rates on retail credit and deposit products.
- There is frequently little or no correlation between retail product and wholesale product rates for pricing assets and liabilities as many retail products are marketing driven and marketing considerations impose restrictions on the repricing of retail products that do not affect wholesale products.
- Retail products frequently include embedded options which are often not rationally exercised, such as the right to prepay certain retail credit products without significant penalties, while wholesale products typically carry penalties for repayment or include rights to terminate wholesale contracts on very different terms than are common in retail products.

There are several reasons why a bank with a significant number of retail customers may find its balance sheet shape and structure difficult to manage. They include:

- Banks with a wide retail base are often driven by relationship considerations and not simply contractual obligations, i.e. they are customer focused.
- Attracting and retaining customers often involves offering retail products whose features are different from wholesale market products, and because of inherent differences in the structure of the different types of products, managing the risk of retail products using tools designed for managing the risk of wholesale products may be difficult.
- Pricing of retail products often has more to do with marketing considerations rather than prevailing market price, which drives the pricing of wholesale products.
- The way retail customers behave in relation to the retail banking products they hold often results in the apparent contractual obligations of the parties providing a poor description of the actual nature of the obligations. For example it may be contractually possible to withdraw funds from a savings account on 30 days' notice, but the customer has a right to leave the money on account indefinitely. The balance on such accounts may behave more like a three-year deposit account than either a 30-day deposit account or a perpetual account.

It is often these inter-related customer and product behavior features that give rise to the need to monitor and manage the stability of net interest income (or present value of the business) and the liquidity of these balances.

EXAMPLE

PromoBank plans to launch a campaign to increase local deposits with a six-month teaser rate. If the campaign is successful, new deposits will be added to the bank's liability structure, but the risk of those deposits will be uncertain. For example, will the deposits be withdrawn once the teaser rate is no longer in effect? Also, will the new depositors have the same average characteristics as the current depositors? Some may hold their deposits longer, due to the inconvenience and cost of changing banks. Others may withdraw the deposits sooner than 6 months, being more sensitive to other banks' competing offers. Or perhaps the new depositor base will have different liquidity needs altogether than the current depositor base.

Because of the uncertainty of depositor retention, PromoBank's current and future exposure to interest rates is unknown and variable.

1.4 ASSET AND LIABILITY MANAGEMENT (ALM) RISK

For many banks, the income stream is dominated by the net interest income (NII) of the bank. NII is the difference between the interest charged on loans (and other assets) and the interest cost of raising deposits (and other liabilities). The current value (net present value) of the stream of NII over time is the major contributor to the value of the bank.

EXAMPLE

Bank M has $100 mm in deposits on which it pays 2% interest, and $20 mm in equity on which it pays no interest. The loan portfolio of $120 mm earns an average rate of 6%. If rates stay the same, the NII will be [120(0.06) – 100(0.02)=] $5.2 mm per year. If the bank is able to earn this in perpetuity, the present value would be [5.2/0.05=] $104 mm at a discount rate of 5%. The present value of NII is an asset of the bank on its economic balance sheet, and the value of the equity balances assets and liabilities.

Table 1: Economic Value of the Bank

BEFORE RATE INCREASE				AFTER RATE INCREASE			
Assets		**Liabilities**		**Assets**		**Liabilities**	
Loans	20	Deposits	100	Loans	120	Deposits	100
PV NII	104	Equity	124	PV NII	84	Equity	104
Economic value of Assets	224	Economic value of financing	224	Economic value of Assets	204	Economic value of financing	204

This table outlining the economic value of the bank is a "balance sheet" that does not record the assets and liabilities of the bank in accounting terms, but rather in economic value terms. Economic value reflects the earnings potential including the market value of the assets. The interest rate change did not impact the recorded book value of the loans, but impacted the earnings capacity of these loans. In fact, if the bank were to divest these loans, the value they would fetch would reflect the earnings they are expected to generate. The interest rate changes typically do not affect the value of the loans recorded on the balance sheet — typically the value of the loan expected to be repaid equals the amount to be lent and is not impacted by changes in interest rates, unless the change in interest rate impacts the probability of repayment. If interest changes were to impact the repayment of the loans, clearly the economic value as well as the accounting value of the loans would change as well. The focus here lies on where the change in interest rate impacts the bank — the change in interest rates impacts the earnings of the bank and thus its economic value and its equity value.

Note that if the deposit rate increased by 1%, income would drop to $4.2 mm and the value of the perpetual cash flows would drop to $84 mm. This implies a 16% drop in equity value for a 1% change in the deposit rate. If the increase in deposit rates were associated with an increase in the equity discount rate, the value would drop even lower.

The example suggests a type of static analysis that ignores risk in NII and its impact on future income volatility and equity value. Ironically, as NII becomes more stable, the forecasted earnings stream of the bank resembles a fixed rate bond, and the present value of that bond fluctuates with interest rates. If a bank were able to create NII that was proportional to short-term rates, it could instead create an income stream resembling a floating rate bond, whose payments were uncertain but whose value was stable.

Table 2: Bank's Objectives

ALM Policy	Impact on Income	Impact on Equity
Stabilize NII	Stable	Risky
Stabilize value	Variable	Stable

The emphasis a bank places on either of the two closely related yet sometimes competing objectives depends on many factors, including

- The ability of the bank to sustain fluctuations in net income
- The bank's tolerance for earnings fluctuations
- The bank's sensitivity to balance sheet ratios
- Shareholder preferences and bank comparables

Since the bank's equity is the difference between its assets and liabilities, most banks will try to balance the risk profile of the assets and liabilities using ALM. In so doing, equity cash flows are less exposed to fluctuations in interest rates. Whether the bank at that point seeks to stabilize earnings or stabilize value is a matter of bank policy and preference.

Fluctuations in Net Income

As interest rates change, loans come due, deposits are withdrawn, and new loans are funded, the bank's net interest income fluctuates. Accordingly, there is a risk that the bank may not be able to cover operating expenses. In a highly volatile interest rate environment, particularly when the level, slope and the curvature of the yield curve changes, the earnings impact can be substantial, and can quickly erode the bank's net interest rate margin. While a bank may be able to sustain an operating deficit for a short period of time, prolonged shortfalls will lead to financial distress for the bank. For this reason, NII stabilization is usually considered the most important aspect of ALM whenever unmanaged NII volatility is too great.

To stabilize the net income, a bank can shift the source of its earnings from interest rate sensitive sources to less interest rate sensitive sources. The primary examples are fees banks charge for underwriting loans, extending different types of credit, and providing services to customers, such as trust, asset management, and trading.

Fluctuations in Earnings

If earnings were the same as income, the issues would be the same. However, accounting rules that require banks to mark various assets and liabilities to market cause fluctuations in the values of assets and liabilities, which must be reported into earnings. For instance, traded assets and liabilities need to be marked-to-market to reflect their fair value. This may be easy to accomplish when the assets are widely traded, reliable price information is available, and markets behave normally, but may be more difficult when price information is less readily available or less reliable.

Variable earnings can lead to unwelcome fluctuations in share value if shareholders make incorrect inferences about value due to reported earnings fluctuations. Also, reduced share value may make it more difficult for banks to grow by acquisition, since the value of their shares as currency in the marketplace is lower.

Sensitivity to Balance Sheet Ratios

Balance sheet ratios based on book values are usually not affected much by changes in interest rates. However, fluctuations in market-value based ratios (such as the market value of debt to equity ratio) can be affected profoundly by interest rate changes. In counterparty trading, the bank requirements to post collateral depend on the strength of its financials. Also, in the various loans to the bank, lines may not be renewed due to adverse balance sheet changes. Balance sheet ratios can affect loan covenants, trigger collateral clauses and cause credit ratings changes. Therefore, if a bank is close to violating a balance sheet constraint, it may run the risk of increasing its operating costs due to increased collateral requirements, and higher interest rates on new debt.

Shareholder Preferences and Bank Comparables

Shareholders may somewhat expect banks to have similar risk profiles, and therefore reward banks to the extent that their risk profiles resemble those of their peers. For example, if all banks stabilized NII, value fluctuations would affect all banks in the same way, causing no surprises for shareholders. Investors could then be indifferent between choosing which banks to invest in. When banks deviate materially from the risk management practices of their peers, they risk having their share price discounted.

1.5 NII RISK IN THE BANKING BOOK

Net interest income is exposed to primarily market risk and secondarily credit risk. Market risk arises from changing interest rates and the repricing of assets and liabilities. The remainder of the section will discuss the impact interest rate changes have on the earnings and value of the bank, or the interest rate in the banking book. Credit risk results from customers defaulting on their loans, which then reduces the bank's earning assets. To understand market risk in the banking book, it is best to begin with a simplified example.

EXAMPLE

HPBank offers its retail customers balloon mortgages at interest rates fixed every five years. This gives customers a mortgage at a fixed repayment rate for a significant period and proves to be popular. A balloon mortgage calls for the payment of interest over a given time period with a final balloon payment required to pay off the mortgage. The balloon mortgage is often replaced with a new balloon mortgage at a repriced rate.

HPBank does not take customer deposits on a similar basis. Most of its deposits have a very short contractual maturity. For example, deposits that may be withdrawn on demand or after 30 days' notice are the bank's most common deposit product. As a result the bank pays a one-month market rate for these deposits.

HPBank is therefore running a business that has a significant amount of interest rate risk. It is receiving the fixed five-year rate from its mortgage customers and paying the one-month rate to its depositors. Unless HPBank's Treasury manages this risk in the wholesale financial markets, if interest rates rise across the yield curve, the bank will have to pay more for its deposits within a period of at most 30 days, but will not be able to increase all its mortgage rates for up to five years.

The actual cost to HPBank will greatly depend on the average time to the repricing of the mortgages. For example, the bank might have made some of these loans four years and 364 days ago and will only have to wait one day to issue a new loan with the higher interest rate. However, it might also have made some of the loans yesterday and therefore would have to wait four years and 364 days before it could raise the interest rate on these loans or charge the higher rate on new loans.

The dangers of not managing interest rate risk in the banking book were highlighted in the example of the American savings and loan crisis.

EXAMPLE

The US savings and loan associations (S&Ls) are essentially mortgage lenders, with the ability in some states to make direct investments to own other businesses and carry out property development.

Until the 1980s they were mainly mutual associations owned by their members; however, as a result of the financial disasters (described below) they are now primarily owned by the US government or by stockholders.

While estimating the total cost of the bailout of the S&Ls is difficult, some reports put the figure as high as USD 500 billion. Although there were instances of fraud, the root cause of the disaster was twofold.

First, mortgages were issued on properties with greatly inflated prices. When the property market collapsed the security on many mortgages was wiped out. Second, although interest rates on a large number of mortgages were fixed, many customers could repay their mortgages early without penalty enabling them to refinance their mortgages at a lower cost when interest rates started to fall. Unfortunately lenders were still locked into paying higher interest rates on the borrowings they raised to fund the original mortgages.

This mismatched position of being locked into paying a higher rate for funds, with the only source of income being new mortgages issued at lower rates, caused many S&Ls to collapse with losses of billions of dollars.

1.5.1 Basic NII Risk Model

In ALM terminology, let's assume HPBank's $200 mm mortgage loan portfolio reprices every 5 years at LIBOR + 2% and its $180 mm in deposits reprice every month at LIBOR – 1%. Its rate sensitive assets (RSA) are the mortgages it holds, or $200 mm. Its rate sensitive liabilities (RSL) are its deposits, or $180 mm. HPBank's repricing gap is defined to be the difference between its rate sensitive assets and its rate sensitive liabilities in a given time bucket. The cumulative gap is the running sum of the periodic gap measures.

For convenience, assume that a constant fraction of the mortgages (i.e. 1/5 of them) mature every year and are replaced with new mortgages. Also assume that while some depositors come and go every month, the level of deposits stays the same.

In this case, if 3-month LIBOR goes up 1% (i.e. mortgage rates and deposit rates), we can expect asset income to rise by 20 basis points in the next year, since only 1/5 of the assets will reprice. The following table shows the repricing schedule for assets and liabilities assuming deposit repricing is effectively instantaneous.

Table 3: Repricing Gap Analysis

Year	0	1	2	3	4	5
Rate sensitive assets — RSA						
Balloon mortgages	0	40	40	40	40	40
Rate sensitive liabilities — RSL						
Deposits	180					
Repricing gap	-180	40	40	40	40	40
Cumulative gap	-180	-140	-100	-60	-20	20

An asset-sensitive bank will show a positive cumulative gap, and a liability-sensitive bank will show a negative cumulative gap. An asset-sensitive bank benefits from rising rates, while a liability-sensitive bank is hurt by rising rates.

The table suggests HPBank is liability-sensitive and will therefore be hurt by rising interest rates. Taken at face value in year 0, HPBank's repricing assets are worth $0 mm and its liabilities $180 mm, then its gap is -$180 mm. This implies that a 1% rate increase now has no impact on mortgage income, but increases the cost of deposits by 1% or $1,800,000. Therefore, every 1% increase in interest rates affects NII adversely by $1,800,000 in year zero. In year 1, 20% of the mortgages reprice, so the additional 1% yield is earned on 1/5th of the mortgage portfolio.

If the 1% increase in rates is permanent, we can expect asset income to eventually be higher by 1%, which will not be enough to cover the $1,800,000 loss per year in deposit interest until year 5. On a present value basis, the 1% increase in interest rates would therefore have a devastating effect on the value of HPBank's equity.

In practice, even the simplest bank would have a much more complicated Repricing Gap Analysis table. However, we have kept the analysis simple to focus on the methodology without being overwhelmed with the details of the repricing structure of all of a bank's assets and liabilities.

1.5.2 Basic NII Risk Management

The bank could reduce its exposure to rising interest rates by doing one of the following:

- Reducing the average repricing time of its loans
- Increasing the average repricing time of its deposits
- Entering into interest rate swaps

Practically speaking, the first two options may be difficult. These options are structural hedges or balance sheet hedges where the bank changes its overall asset and liability composition. The first could be accomplished by offering adjustable-rate mortgages instead of fixed-rate mortgages, but the bank might find the demand for its mortgages is lower as a result. The second could be accomplished by offering depositors CDs (certificates of deposit) with higher rates for longer deposit terms, but most depositors prefer to keep their accounts liquid, and available immediately. In addition, the higher interest rates paid will affect profitability.

The third option is an example of a financial hedge. Here the bank could enter into an interest rate swap agreement wherein it would receive floating payments and pay fixed payments. In this type of swap arrangement, the increased payments of the swap would offset the losses to NII. Conversely, when NII were high because of falling rates, HPBank would have higher compensating NII income.

Hedging with Interest Rate Swaps

Continuing with the HP bank example, suppose the bank were to enter a fixed-for-floating interest rate swap linked to LIBOR, i.e. pay fixed interest in exchange for floating interest at time zero. In particular, the swap would be structured as five swaps, each swap with a $40 mm notional amount, and maturities ranging from 1 to 5 years.

The logic of this approach is to take the fixed payments on the mortgages and replace them with an index-linked equivalent. Also, since each swap can be represented as selling a fixed rate bond and buying a floating rate bond (see Chapter 3 for further detail on this analogy), it is simple to incorporate into the repricing table:

Table 4: Repricing Gap Analysis with Swap

Year	0	1	2	3	4	5
Rate sensitive assets — RSA						
Balloon mortgages	0	40	40	40	40	40
Swap floating side	200					
Rate sensitive liabilities — RSL						
Deposits	180					
Swap fixed side		40	40	40	40	40
Repricing gap	20	0	0	0	0	0
Cumulative gap	20	20	20	20	20	20

The result appears to be appealing, completely eliminating the repricing gap. However, while the interest rate swap is the simplest and most popular ALM management tool, it has its own problems associated with it. As discussed in Chapter 3 of the *Market Risk Management* book in the *GARP Risk Series*, the swap creates counterparty risk and margining risk, which may be difficult for HPBank to manage. Also, if the NII risk model assumptions are incorrect, a swap may overhedge or underhedge the risk.

For example, suppose that rates dropped and many mortgages refinanced. If twice the mortgages refinanced in the first year than expected, and the remaining evenly distributed mortgages refinanced on schedule, the resulting Repricing Gap Analysis would show:

Table 5: Repricing Gap Analysis with Swap After Rates Collapse

Year	0	1	2	3	4	5
Rate sensitive assets — RSA						
Balloon Mortgages	0	80	30	30	30	30
Swap floating side	200					
Rate sensitive liabilities — RSL						
Deposits	180					
Swap fixed side		40	40	40	40	40
Repricing gap	20	40	-10	-10	-10	-10
Cumulative gap	20	60	50	40	30	20

The positive cumulative gap shows that the bank was not hedged with the plain vanilla interest rate swap; rather, it overhedged because it assumed no refinancing (i.e. repayments) of the mortgages. Ironically, the simple hedge moved the bank from being liability-sensitive to being asset-sensitive.

1.5.3 Critiques of the Basic NII Risk Model

There are four major critiques of the basic NII risk model, most of which can be addressed using more advanced models. None of them completely eliminates model risk or the risk of overhedging or underhedging NII risk. The major critiques are concerned with differential interest rate sensitivities, the calculation of effective repricing dates, the lack of a link to the amount of funds intermediated and the lack of measurement of change in market value. These are all explained below.

Differential Interest Rate Sensitivities

Assets and liabilities of the same repricing period need not have the same sensitivity to interest rate changes. For example, if mortgage rates are linked to one interest rate index and deposit rates don't have a one-to-one relationship, or correlation, to interest rate changes, a model that treats the interest rate sensitivities as being the same will misstate the NII interest rate risk. For instance, many banks price their loans off a prime rate pricing grid, where the credit quality of the customer affects the margin paid above or below that prime rate. A higher rated customer with lower default risk would pay below prime rate and a low rated customer, with a higher default risk would pay a premium above the prime rate. Deposits, on the other hand, are priced either off the inter-bank market for the larger banks and the local interest rate levels for smaller banks. As large banks compete for large corporate and other institutional deposits, these deposits are often priced close to what other larger banks pay in the interbank market. Thus, changes in the deposit rates offered by the larger banks often reflect yield changes in the interbank market. Smaller banks that are less able to compete for institutional deposits and rely more on retail deposits and smaller corporate deposits for their funding, often price their deposits in competition with other smaller banks.

This shortcoming is normally addressed using historical regression analysis to determine the relationship between asset rates and interest rates, and between deposit rates and interest rates. However, as bank strategies change, the relationship between earning assets and funding liabilities, including the earnings spread changes,and as a result the analytical results may provide incorrect results.

Also, rate sensitivities at different maturities will almost surely differ. For example, a given change in the 3-month LIBOR rate will have a different effect on short-term deposit rates and long-term time deposit and CD rates. This shortcoming can be addressed by estimating the historical impact of 3-month LIBOR on the two rates in question, or using a different, more long-term, index base to model the pricing structure.

Effective Repricing Dates

As we saw in the earlier HPBank example, while a 5-year fixed rate mortgage that converts to an adjustable mortgage has a maximum repricing period of 5 years, its expected repricing period is shorter due to the possibility of prepayment, i.e. early repayment of the loan. If customers repaid their loans randomly, this would not create problems for large banks, but in fact, customers repay their loans more frequently when interest rates fall, because they can secure alternative financing, refinancing, at a lower cost. For a bank, which normally would benefit from falling rates, this could be a disaster — the repricing period of the assets falls precisely when interest rates fall, prompting increasing early repayments, further weakening the bank's NII.

Banks combat the weakening NII due to interest rate changes differently. One widely used approach is to penalize those borrowers who want to repay their loans early. As long as the penalty is substantial enough and is enforceable, the incentive for borrowers to refinance at a lower cost is reduced or prohibited on economic grounds. Another alternative is to extend the loans with terms that clearly prohibit early repayment of the loan, or allow only partial early repayment of loans.

Deposits have the opposite tendency. While contractually, depositors are not required to keep liquid funds on deposit for very long, in fact, they tend to leave their deposits for longer periods of time, even if interest rates rise and the bank does not raise its deposit interest rate. This phenomenon is called deposit "stickiness." These deposits are considered to be the bank's "core deposits" and play an important function in the funding of the bank. As these core deposits are non-interest rate sensitive and are kept in the bank for extended time periods, correctly identifying these deposits and assessing their size is one of the important functions a successful ALM function must achieve.

The effective repricing period for HPBank's deposits may be a year even though the contractual repricing period is a month. If this is the case, HPBank would temporarily benefit from increases in interest rates if it kept its deposit rate the same while enjoying higher income on its repriced loans. However, if the bank does this for a long time, it can expect to see erosion in its depositor base.

Typically, larger commercial deposit customers and more sophisticated retail deposit customers move their deposits to accounts that momentarily earn higher yields. Once these depositors start to move their core deposits at a larger scale, the bank should counter by offering more competitive rates to these customers. Oftentimes, relatively higher interest rates offered on larger and longer maturity time deposits reduce these customers' yield maximizing behavior.

Link to Amount of Intermediated Funds

The simple NII model treats assets and liabilities as if the amounts were unaffected by changes in interest rates. As we saw in the last paragraphs, however, changes in rates affect the number of loans outstanding and the amount of deposits held. To estimate the bank's true NII sensitivity to interest rate changes it is necessary to consider the impact of rate changes on asset and liability levels.

The complexity lies in the diverging direction of the two feedback loops. Lower interest rates fuel increasing lending activity, which given the bank's capital position, can increase the bank's earning assets. Lower interest rates can also fuel early repayments, particularly retail. These early repayments reduce earning assets, the yield on earning assets and the net interest margin. Lower interest rates also reduce the risk that borrowers default. And finally, lower interest rates reduce the bank's funding costs.

Higher interest rates lead to higher earnings yield for the bank with attendant higher costs to fund its assets. Higher interest rates reduce the incentives of prepayment, but also introduce the added risk that financially struggling weak borrowers may not be able to continue to make higher interest payments in a timely manner with defaults and loss of earning assets to follow. Moreover, the higher interest rates could prompt depositors to shift their funds to bank deposits, further increasing the bank's funding costs.

Change in Market Value

The strongest criticism of the NII risk model is that while it considers risk to income, it does not consider risk related to changes in the value of market values of assets and liabilities as mentioned above. Hence, no ALM risk report is complete without measures of both NII risk and value risk. The changes in market values and earnings capacity ultimately affect the equity value of the bank. This type of risk is often called equity risk, since it has to do with risk to the changes in assets minus liabilities. Equity risk measurement using duration is the subject of the next section.

1.6 EQUITY RISK IN THE BANKING BOOK

Historically, although the banking book is largely not marked-to-market, and its value is adjusted to the expected recovery on the loans included in that book, risk managers have wanted to know how changes in interest rates impact the net value of the bank's assets and liabilities. The purpose of this exercise is to understand the longer-term impact, outside of short-term earnings fluctuations, of rising or falling rates on the bank.

Since future assets and liabilities are priced to market when they are incepted — the loans are underwritten and funded, the investment securities purchased, and the deposits made, they are not affected by changes in today's interest rates. They are affected by the future level of interest rates. Therefore, we may concentrate on the current portfolio of assets and liabilities, and determine how sensitive it is to changes in interest rates. The most widely tool used for this purpose is the modified duration, which was introduced in Chapter 3 of the Market Risk Management book in *the GARP Risk Series*. By way of review, the modified duration of a bond is the estimated percentage drop in the value of the bond per 1% rise in yield.

The change in the equity of the bank for a change in interest rates can therefore be written as:

Change in equity value of the bank =
- (Modified duration of assets x Value of assets
- Modified duration of liabilities x Value of liabilities)
x Increase in average yield

When divided by the value of the assets of the bank, the term in parentheses is known as the duration gap. The duration gap measures the percentage sensitivity of the bank's assets per 1% change in yields.

EXAMPLE

HPBank (above) had \$200 mm in loans and \$180 mm in deposits. If the modified duration of the loans is estimated to be 3, and the modified duration of the deposits is estimated to be 1, then the change in HPBank's equity value per 1% change in yield is:

Change in equity value =
-(3 x 200 – 1 x 180) x 1% = -\$4.2 mm per 1% change in yield

The duration gap is (3 x 200 – 1 x 180)/200 or 2.1% per 1% change in yield.

1.6.1 Hedging Equity Risk

Equity risk can also be hedged using interest rate swaps. Interest rate swaps, as mentioned above, insulate the bank's NII from certain fluctuations in interest rates. Since the variability of interest rates and NII are both reduced, the residual equity value is stabilized as well. Using interest rate swaps to reduce the effect of variability of interest rates is sometimes called **immunization**. To reduce the variability of NII, the bank enters into swap positions that make the bank's duration gap equal to zero. That is, after immunization, a bank's equity should in theory not be sensitive to changes in interest rates.

In the case of HPBank above, it would need to enter interest rate swaps where it was paying fixed and receiving floating in order to get its duration to zero. From this point of view, the bank itself looks like a swap position (long fixed assets and short floating liabilities), so to reverse its risk it must take the opposite swap position in the marketplace.

The difference between NII hedging and equity hedging is straightforward. NII hedging matches repricing risk in assets and liabilities to produce a stable income stream. This can be achieved by structural or financial hedges. Equity hedging, if successful, converts the NII into cash flows into payments that resemble a floating rate bond — whose present value remains immune to changes in interest rates.

1.6.2 Critiques of the Duration Gap Model

In general, the criticisms of duration as a risk measure apply to criticisms of duration-based gap management. These include the dynamic nature of the calculation, the costs of immunization, errors in the linear model and basis risk. Since all of these issues were addressed in Chapter 3 of the Market Risk Management book in *the GARP Risk Series,* they are covered only briefly here.

Dynamic Calculation

Duration is not constant, and changes as a function of time and as a function of yields. Any duration-matching strategy is necessarily short-term in nature and needs to be adjusted frequently to be effective. The dynamic nature of duration calculation has practical implications. As the various hedges come due — swap contracts mature, assets and liabilities mature to be replaced with new assets and liabilities, the shape and structure of the yield curve shifts — the bank has to roll some of the hedges forward. Herein is the risk that hedges may not be perfectly rolled forward or the cost of hedging may actually exceed the benefits it may provide, reducing their practical application.

Costs of Immunization

Because of the need to hedge dynamically, the changing hedge position creates trading costs and managerial difficulty as mentioned above. Cheaper strategies may be devised that meet the bank's risk management objectives but are not as costly to execute; however, all trading based strategies inherently assume the risks associated with the roll.

Errors in the Linear Model

Duration models assume the percentage change in price per 1% change in yield is constant, but this is incorrect, since the price functions are nonlinear. To some extent, this can be corrected using convexity, but this increases dependence on the assumption of parallel shifts in the yield curve — a questionable assumption.

Basis Risk

Yields changes are not uniform. Changes in market rates affect different time buckets differently and they affect asset and liability yields differently. As such, a "beta-adjusted" duration gap that reflected these differences might perform better. For example, if the municipal bond index changes 88 bp for every 100 bp change in LIBOR, the hedge ratios for muni-related risks would be the same as LIBOR hedges, except they are multiplied by 0.88 to reflect the reduced risk of munis.

1.7 CONCLUSIONS

While bank treasuries operate differently in some regards, most take primary responsibility for managing the ALM risk of the bank. This involves drawing a balance between stabilizing net income and stabilizing bank equity value, often competing objectives.

The main determinant of a bank's sensitivity to interest rate changes is its repricing structure. Asset-sensitive banks reprice their assets quickly, and benefit from rising rates, while liability-sensitive banks reprice their liabilities quickly and benefit from falling rates. A bank's repricing schedule is extremely difficult to determine. Some contractual assets, like mortgages, will vary in size (via prepayment changes) as interest rates change. The same is true of some liabilities, such as deposits, even though those are not contractual in nature. The Repricing Gap Analysis tables presented in this chapter do not begin to approach the complexity of actual bank exposures.

Once the bank has modeled its assets and liabilities, it may choose to alter its exposure to interest rates using structural hedges or financial hedges. Structural hedges require a change in bank strategy to increase or decrease various types of assets or liabilities. Financial hedges are usually complex portfolios of interest rate swaps. Both types of hedges can be costly, in terms of execution and in terms of producing undesired consequences.

This chapter has explored the basic problems associated with interest rate risk in ALM, but has not addressed advanced issues related to accounting, incentives or regulatory capital impact. The student is encouraged to explore this field in greater depth upon completion of this volume.

1.8 SUMMARY

This chapter has introduced a number of key concepts and issues involved in treasury risk management. Students should review this summary before proceeding.

The Role of the Treasury

- The role of a Treasury in a bank varies greatly depending on the business model adopted by the bank.
- For banks with a commercial/retail focus the Treasury is likely to manage the net interest rate risk in their banking book directly with market counterparties by operating a trading desk.
- If a bank has substantial commercial and retail business, and the currency in which it primarily operates is not a major currency, then in practice it may run interest rate risk positions for profit.

- Where a commercial and retail bank operates in a heavily traded currency it is likely that its treasury operation will be primarily focused on ensuring that the risks generated by the bank's businesses are covered in the market. Such treasury operations are commonly known as cover operations.
- Cover operations make sure that the profits generated by the customer business are not damaged by the failure to manage the inherent market risk (e.g., the interest rate risk in the banking book).
- For banks with an investment banking operation actively engaged in traded market risk and managing it for profit, the Treasury function is likely to be primarily concerned with the effective transfer of interest rate risk in the banking book to the investment bank at a fair transfer price.

The Nature of Treasury Risk

- Treasury risk is defined as the risk of loss in the activities of a bank's Treasury and therefore depends on the risk management function of the Treasury itself.
- While treasury functions can vary from bank to bank, they normally include the management of risks such as interest rate risk in the banking book and liquidity risk.

Asset and Liability Management

- Asset and liability management is usually governed by the Asset Liability Committee (ALCO) or the risk management committee.
- Asset and liability management in most banks has the primary objective of managing interest rate risk in the bank's balance sheet and ensuring that the interest rate risk inherent in the bank's underlying business does not disrupt the production of a stable income stream over time.
- A second objective of ALM is to manage risk to the bank's equity due to changes in interest rates.
- The emphasis a bank places on either of the two (very closely related) objectives — managing risk or stabilizing business value — often depends on shareholder expectations and the management accounting practices that it follows.
- Management accounting practices are often heavily influenced by the financial accounting standards followed by the country where the bank is incorporated.
- ALM can be compared to bond portfolio management. Although it has some similar characteristics, the problem is fundamentally different.
- The repricing structure of assets and liabilities changes constantly, both for interest-rate related reasons and for behavioral reasons (e.g. prepayment of loans and withdrawal of deposits).
- Marketing and strategic considerations also affect ALM risk estimates.

ALM Risk

- Net interest income (NII) is the difference between interest earned on assets and liabilities.
- Fluctuations in NII are driven by the repricing of assets and liabilities.
- Earnings risk differs from NII risk, but is harder to measure due to accounting conventions.
- Accounting balance sheet ratios are mostly static, but economic balance sheet valuations can change dramatically as rates change.

NII Risk

- The Repricing Gap Analysis table groups assets and liabilities by expected maturity bucket. Until an asset or liability reprices, i.e. resets its fixed rate to new market rates, it presents interest rate risk.
- The repricing gap is the value (by bucket) of repriced assets minus repriced liabilities.
- The cumulative repricing gap is the running sum of the individual repricing gaps. An asset-sensitive bank is one with positive cumulative repricing gaps, while a liability-sensitive bank has negative cumulative repricing gaps.
- A bank can hedge NII risk with plain vanilla interest rate swaps, but runs the risk of over or under-hedging if the underlying asset and liability repricing schedule changes as rates change.
- The basic NII model is criticized on the basis that (a) assets and liabilities have different interest rate sensitivities, (b) effective repricing dates can be different than contractual repricing dates, (c) the amount of intermediated funds can be a function of interest rate levels and (d) NII risk does not address the impact of changing interest rates on bank equity value.

Equity Risk in the Banking Book

- The change in the equity value of the bank can be estimated using duration of assets and liabilities.
- If a bank wanted to neutralize its equity to changes in interest rates, it could also use interest rate swaps.
- Most banks do not focus primarily on this risk.
- Other problems include (a) the duration measure is dynamic, (b) immunization against risk can be costly, (c) the linear model used to estimate duration is approximate and does not reflect large changes in rates and (d) not all rates rise and fall 1-1 with interest rate indices.

Chapter 2

Liquidity Risk in the Banking Book

In this chapter, we focus on how banks manage liquidity risk, that is, the potential short-term cash demands that can be placed upon banks by depositors, borrowers, the bank's own borrowing activities, trading activities and counterparty interactions. Liquidity squeezes leave banks vulnerable to potential default on their obligations, and in some cases trigger bankruptcy. Because liquidity demands are difficult to predict in advance, they present an important risk to bank managers. This risk is usually managed by the bank's treasury as part of the asset and liability management function.

On completion of this chapter the reader will have a basic understanding of:

- Sources and uses of liquidity
- Types and drivers of liquidity risk
- Add-on costs of liquidity risk
- The relationship between liquidity risk and the credit crisis of 2007-9
- Liquidity risk measurement issues
- Liquidity risk management alternatives
- Best practices in liquidity risk management
- Liquidity risk reporting

This chapter focuses on funding liquidity risk — the ability of the bank to fund its obligations when they come due. Funding liquidity risk is different from transactional or trading liquidity risk — the ability to trade in markets without significant price concessions, or risk of an increase in a security's bid-offer spread or reduction in market depth for a traded security — which was covered in Chapter 6 of the Market Risk Management book in *the GARP Risk Series*. To meet funding liquidity needs, banks may establish holdings of highly liquid assets that they expect to sell, with a short notice, to raise funds when they need them. Thus the funding liquidity risk can become related to trading liquidity risk, but these two different types of risks are not the same.

2.1 INTRODUCTION TO LIQUIDITY RISK

Liquidity risk is the risk of not being able to meet obligations when they fall due. The chief day-to-day liquidity obligations that are specific to banks are two-fold: the ability to fund deposit withdrawals as depositors redeem their deposits and the ability to fund loan drawdowns when the bank's borrowers need to have access to the lent funds. Apart from these two bank-specific liquidity obligations, banks encounter the standard liquidity obligation of paying their bills and other debts in a contractual and timely manner.

This mostly becomes problematic for banks when their liquidity requirements are not known in advance. That is, some liabilities have scheduled repayment amounts and dates and can be predicted easily. One important liability, future deposit levels, cannot be predicted with certainty. Other liabilities, such as those created by counterparty failure or market risk in leveraged cash or derivative positions, cannot be forecasted accurately and therefore can have a significant effect on liquidity requirements.

Examples of bank events that can stress liquidity include:

- Obligations to fund assets (e.g. mortgages)
- Maturing of bank debt
- Unusually large depositor withdrawals (potential precursor to a bank run)
- Nonperforming assets (causing cash shortfalls)
- Exercise of customer put provisions requiring a bank to repurchase assets
- Repurchase agreements
- Futures margins
- Counterparty collateral calls (and failure of counterparties to supply collateral)

In one way or another, liquidity risk has affected every financial institution in the credit crisis that started in 2008. The first major failure of a financial institution in the US was Bear Stearns in March 2008. Bear Stearns was not a commercial bank, but an investment — merchant — bank, and as such faced broader strategic alternatives than commercial banks that are more heavily regulated and face a more limited range of strategic choices.

EXAMPLE[1]

A sudden surge of "broad cash outflows" from counterparties and customers on Thursday forced Bear Stearns to tap JP Morgan Chase and the Federal Reserve for funds to shore up liquidity, the investment bank's chief executive said Friday.

During a hastily convened conference call, CEO Alan Schwartz said the bank continued to have very strong liquidity in the first part of the week, but demands from prime brokerage clients, repo clients, and lenders to cash out late Thursday forced the move. Said CFO Sam Molinaro: "Counterparties that were providing secured financing against assets were no longer willing to provide financing. We lost a lot of capacity." At the pace funds were being withdrawn, the firm recognized that there could be continued liquidity demands that would "outstrip our resources," said Schwartz.

Eventually, Bear Stearns' resources were outstripped and the bank was bought by JPMorgan Chase in a transaction shepherded by the US Government. Had Bear Stearns been able to meet their exceptional liquidity demands, they would not have been forced to sell their assets to another bank, and would likely still be in business today.

Under ordinary circumstances, liquidity demands are met routinely in the normal course of business. When a bank struggles to meet its obligations, it may use the endogenous liquidity of the assets, the exogenous liquidity of the bank's balance sheet, or the contingent liquidity of another financial institution's balance sheet. These three types of liquidity are explained below.

2.1.1 Types of Liquidity

There are three different concepts of liquidity: endogenous liquidity, exogenous liquidity and external liquidity.

Endogenous liquidity is the liquidity inherent in the banks' assets themselves. Assets exhibit various forms of endogenous liquidity:

- Related to the ability to sell the asset in a liquid market rapidly, and at a bid/offer spread (the difference between the price to the buyer and seller of the asset) that is small and minimally affected by the size of the transaction.
- Related to the maturity of the asset. A loan with a one-week duration has far greater natural liquidity than a ten-year loan.
- Related to the quality of the asset. A 30-year U.S. Treasury bond is more liquid than a 30-year prime mortgage, which is typically even more liquid than a 3-year sub-prime mortgage.

Typically, government issued or backed securities exhibit the greatest endogenous liquidity.

Exogenous liquidity (often called funding liquidity) is the liquidity provided by the bank's liability structure to fund its assets and maturing liabilities.

Exogenous liquidity is particularly important when the assets of a bank cannot be readily sold (a situation for many commercial and retail banks). Clearly a bank that lends illiquid ten-year loans and funds itself entirely on the overnight interbank market is very vulnerable to any refusal by other banks to provide funds. Such a bank would have an extreme mismatch between its asset and liability funding structure, because the funding can dry up immediately.

Liquidity mismatches can cause serious problems as was highlighted by the crisis at Long-Term Capital Management (LTCM), a US hedge fund (see example below). As a hedge fund LTCM depended on the endogenous liquidity of its assets to secure financing. It relied on the equity provided by its investors and the funds it was able to source from debt markets. As a hedge fund LTCM was not allowed to raise deposits as banks can, but was able to secure short-term loans from banks and institutional investors, including banks and other hedge funds.

In this case rather than selling the assets it pledged them as collateral against short-dated loans. A period of severe market disruption in September 1998 meant that LTCM was unable to readily sell or pledge assets in order to obtain shorter-term funding. This was because lenders were concerned at the asset values which were very sensitive to rising interest rates. LTCM wasn't capable of carrying the assets of its business on its balance sheet because it did not have the necessary funding structure.

EXAMPLE

In September 1998 Long-Term Capital Management (LTCM) was rescued from collapse by 16 major counterparties that had agreed to invest USD 4 billion to enable it to 'wind down' its USD 200 billion market exposure in an orderly fashion.[2]

LTCM's capital was mainly provided by banks, permitting the investors to 'gear up', i.e. borrow and make massive returns on a small equity basis from comparatively small price movements. Unlike other investment vehicles which could borrow money only to a limited extent, LTCM was able to borrow many times the amount of its own capital which ultimately led to its near-collapse.

By August 1998, three quarters of LTCM's total notional derivatives exposure of more than USD 1 trillion was in the form of interest rate swaps with some 50 counterparties worldwide, none of whom knew the extent of LTCM's overall exposure. Bear Stearns, the Wall Street firm handling LTCM's settlements, 'pulled the plug' on the company initially by calling in a USD 500 million payment that LTCM was unable to meet because of its inability to sell supposedly highly liquid assets, such as foreign government bonds, in such large volumes.

As a direct result of the LTCM crisis many trading businesses now ensure that they have better access to long-term funding through instruments such as committed funding lines (i.e., commercial bank commitments to lend to them).

External liquidity is the noncontractual and contingent capital supplied by investors and other institutions to support the bank in times of liquidity stress. External liquidity can also refer to the "lender of last resort," for example, the liquidity supplied by central banks in times of crisis. This capital is contingent on an unexpected liquidity need and is typically supplied during times of crisis using various approaches that are available to banks, institutions, and the central bank. It may include repos, discount window borrowings, or other approaches to provide liquidity — cash — to banks when so prompted by a stress event.

While external liquidity in part relates to the financial strength of the bank, or its exogenous liquidity, part also relates to the willingness of third parties to support a bank's liquidity needs. This support can come from lenders or shareholders but can also come from government sources.

Lenders, including other banks, can provide credit lines that are drawn when needed to meet cash needs. When explicit credit lines don't exist, implicit lines sometimes exist. Investors or governments that have a vested interest is rescuing financial institutions have turned out to be the greatest providers of contingent capital to support bank liquidity requirements.

EXAMPLE

Warren Buffett purchased $5 billion of preferred shares from Goldman Sachs in September 2008, and acquired additional options as part of the package. This was a source of implicit external liquidity that was contracted in advance. However, the capital was obtained at a high cost (10% interest plus warrants). Had Goldman been able to contract for contingent liquidity in advance, it would likely have been cheaper.

2.1.2 Sources of Liquidity Problems

Liquidity is essentially a short-term problem. Most liquidity problems are indeed caused by short-term unexpected liabilities, but they can also caused by the funding requirements of long-term liabilities. Liquidity risk therefore arises from (a) the variability in short-term assets and liabilities and (b) the short-term components of long-term assets and liabilities.

EXAMPLE

Many banks use an "originate to distribute" model of mortgage banking. A mortgage is issued, warehoused in the bank, and sold together with other mortgages in a pool. These banks need liquidity to fund mortgages, which usually comes in the form of cash, warehouse loans and sale proceeds. They also take the risk that mortgage values drop or the demand for mortgage-backed securities fall. Even though the mortgages are long-term in nature, therefore, they create short-term liquidity issues for banks.

On the asset side, securities may default or their values may fall. These types of impairment do not cause liquidity problems — the loss in market value affects the accounting treatment of these securities in the financial statements only. However, there is a very important exception in case the impaired security was bought with leverage. To maintain the loan to value ratio between the loan and the security collateralized by the loan, lenders to the bank making the purchase of the impaired security may make margin calls and demand posting of additional collateral in support the transaction. Also, if the security was used as collateral in a trading position, trading counterparties may make collateral calls, stressing the liquidity of the bank because additional collateral demands are typically met through otherwise liquid securities. This is a vicious circle — the declining values lead to additional collateral and leads to additional liquidity demands, which in turn lead to further declining asset values as the following picture illustrates.

Figure 1: "Vicious Asset Circle"

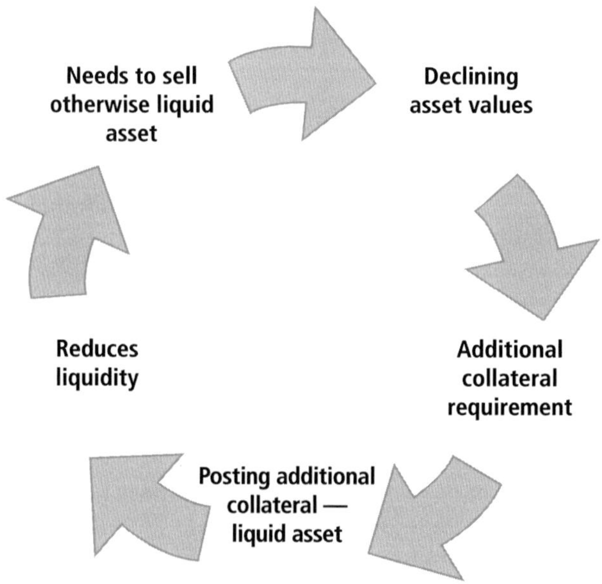

In the case of a commercial bank, when depositors demand their funds, they are converting longer-term bank liabilities into shorter-term liabilities. In a classical "bank run," the short-term liabilities exceed the available liquid assets of the bank, and the bank is forced into liquidating assets, restructuring, or going bankrupt.[3]

Some sources of liquidity risk are not as obvious as loan funding and depositor runs on the bank. A complete liquidity risk assessment would require a bank to examine its repurchase agreements, futures margins and OTC trading activities, to determine if its sources of liquidity and contingent funding were sufficient to meet extreme scenarios.

Repurchase Agreements

A repurchase agreement, or "Repo" uses a security as collateral to obtain a loan. The counterparty sells the securities to the lender and agrees to repurchase them at a later date at a fixed price or interest rate formula, allowing the lender to earn a rate of return on the loan. The loan amount is typically less than the value of the security by a percentage *haircut,* which can be quite small for government securities or quite large for very risky securities.

Repos behave like margin loans except that the implicit leverage is much greater. Since the lender takes significant risk in these transactions, they reserve the right to change the interest rate formula, the amount of the haircut or other credit terms to increase their margin calls when they feel it is appropriate. For example, the lender may reserve the right to increase margin calls if a counterparty's credit rating declines. Collectively, these features can lead to rapidly rising liquidity demands in times of financial distress.

EXAMPLE

A bank enters a short-term repo transaction wherein it sells $100 million in CDOs with the agreement to repurchase the CDOs with interest. Because of the risk of the instruments, the counterparty normally applies a 20% haircut, so that the bank is able to effectively borrow $80 million. As the value of CDOs fell during the credit crisis, haircuts for CDOs increased, and some counterparties would not lend at all on CDOs, either of which could have dramatically affected the bank's availability of funds.

Futures Margins

Banks often trade on futures exchanges to reduce their market risk and counterparty credit risk. Market risk is reduced by taking hedge positions, and credit risk is reduced by transacting with a well-capitalized exchange. However, in giving up market and credit risk, the bank assumes a great deal of liquidity risk in its futures contracting activities. Since cash demands must be met on a one-day notice,[4] banks can find themselves scrambling for funds, faced with the prospect of liquidating a losing position, selling other assets to raise cash, or finding other sources of short-term liquidity. Failing these remedies, banks could go bankrupt as a result of their hedging operations.

Futures margins may vary with prices, but exchange margin requirements can also change unexpectedly, either for individual contracts or for futures portfolios. This is an additional source of risk to futures hedgers and speculators alike.

OTC Collateral Calls

Over-the-counter derivative positions that move against a counterparty in excess of their credit lines usually require collateral to be posted. They can behave like futures margins when the derivative positions resemble futures contracts. They can also behave like repurchase agreements in some cases. Therefore, all the liquidity risks affecting repos and futures apply to OTC contracts as well.

In short, nearly all of the bank's assets and liabilities have some liquidity risk associated with them. Some liquidity risks are predictable and well-known in advance, while other risks are unknown in both time and size. This can lead in some cases to incredible cash demands on the bank. If a bank is otherwise healthy, an increase in cash demands can be met by additional short-term borrowing. However, if many banks experience difficulties at the same time, the reduction in available funds to all banks can have disastrous consequences as have taken place in 2008-9.

2.1.3 Costs of Mismanaging Liquidity Risk

Liquidity risk extends beyond the potential inability to fund obligations. When a bank's sources of liquidity dry up, the bank may not be able to operate further without external assistance. When a bank has to sell its assets or go bankrupt, it incurs many add-on losses in addition. These losses include:

- The discount accepted by the bank for selling its assets in a "fire sale"
- The increased cost of funding liabilities in a financially distressed situation
- Reduction in the value of reputation, good will and present value of future growth opportunities in the event of financial distress
- The loss of all good will and intangible assets (e.g. reputation and customer relationships) in the event of a bankruptcy

The credit crisis of 2007-9 has demonstrated that even the largest financial institutions are vulnerable to liquidity risk. The table below shows a sample of firms affected by liquidity management problems.

Table 1: A Sample of Firms Affected by Liquidity Management

Date	Place	Event
Feb. 2008	UK	Nationalization of Northern Rock
Mar. 2008	US	Collapse of Bear Stearns
July 2008	US	IndyMac Bancorp seized by federal regulators
Sept. 2008	US	Federal takeover of Fannie Mae and Freddie Mac
Sept. 2008	Germany	Commerzbank buys Dresdner
Sept. 2008	US	WaMu seized by U.S. and assets sold to JPMorgan
Sept. 2008	US	Bankruptcy of Lehman Brothers
Sept. 2008	US	Wells Fargo acquisition of Wachovia
Oct. 2008	Iceland	Nationalization of all its major banks
Oct. 2008	Netherlands	Nationalization of Dutch part of Fortis
Oct. 2008	US	Merrill Lynch taken over by Bank of America
Nov. 2008	Latvia	Takeover of Parex after run on the bank
Jan. 2009	Belgium	KBC gets state support
Jan. 2009	Ireland	Nationalization of Anglo Irish Bank

While nationalization or bankruptcy is one extreme outcome of poor liquidity management, this table does not list the thousands of financial institutions that were severely impacted by the crisis. Many of these institutions were able to survive through a combination of asset sales, cost cutting and capital infusion, but nearly all have seen their share prices collapse.

Liquidity problems existed long before the credit crisis. In a Fitch Ratings Special Report, Fitch Bank Failures Study 1990-2003, banks globally experienced a cumulative failure rate of 5.52%. However, the actual cumulative default rate was 0.48%, suggesting that the majority (94%) of these banks were supported or bailed out before they ever defaulted. While this would seem beneficial from the point of view of systemic risk, we can conclude bank managers at failing banks have not done as well.[5]

2.2 LIQUIDITY RISK MEASUREMENT

To measure a bank's aggregate liquidity, it is important to model each of the assets and liabilities that make up a bank's balance sheet. Each asset and liability has cash flow impact associated with it — origination, purchase, dividends, coupons, interest, default and redemption or sale. Some assets and liabilities lend themselves easily to quantitative models, while others are more difficult. This section discusses the classic static liquidity analysis, the liquidity ladder, and its extension into probabilistic liquidity models.

2.2.1 Static Model — The Liquidity Ladder

At any point in time, a bank will typically model its liquidity requirements using a liquidity ladder. The liquidity ladder is used by banks for active liquidity management out to a few months at most, but some banks also derive longer-term liquidity ladders to identify weaknesses in their liquidity structure.

The liquidity ladder is a statement of cash flow sources and uses. A simple liquidity ladder for a bank one day in the future might be composed as follows:

Table 2: A Simple Liquidity Ladder

Day 1		
Sources of Cash	**Use of Cash**	**Net Cash Requirement**
Maturing assets	Maturing contractual liabilities	
Interest receivable	Interest payable	
Asset sales	Deposit runoffs	
Bank's drawdown on credit lines	Customer drawdown of bank lines	
Total sources	**Total uses**	**Net = Sources - Uses**

The liquidity ladder is similar to the framework the bank uses for calculating its duration and repricing gap, with one fundamental difference. The liquidity ladder looks at the timing and the direction of the cash flows, while the framework for the duration gap analysis looks at the valuation points and not those points when the value of the various assets are realized.

The one day liquidity ladder considers contractual payment dates of assets and liabilities, but also incorporates clearing and settlement features of all the bank's assets and liabilities. For example, an asset sale today would typically lead to cash settlement in the next 2-3 days. If the bank were depending on that cash to meet an obligation today, it would likely end up defaulting.

If a bank discovered its one-day liquidity gap were negative, it could try to shift some of its assets into overnight loans, but this may be difficult if the assets were illiquid or the settlements were delayed. For this reason, the bank manages its liquidity ladder by looking several days into the future. The summary table might look as follows:

Table 3: Liquidity Summary Table

Day(s)	Total sources	Total uses	Net liquidity	Cumulative
1	—	—	—	—
2	—	—	—	—
3-15	—	—	—	—
1	—	—	—	—

Wherever net liquidity was negative, the bank could shift its assets and liabilities to fill the funding gap.

EXAMPLE

Uri Bank has $1 million in cash $20 million in loans coming due tomorrow with an expected default rate of 2%. The proceeds will be deposited overnight. The bank owes $8 million on a securities purchase that settles in two days, and pays off $13 million in commercial paper in three days that is not expected to renew. This is Uri Bank's current liquidity ladder (without overnight lending):

Table 4: Uri Bank liquidity ladder

Day(s)	Total sources	Total uses	Net liquidity	Cumulative
1	\$20.6	\$20.6	\$20.6	\$20.6
2	\$0.0	\$8.0	(8.0)	12.6
3	\$0.0	\$13.0	(13.0)	(0.4)

The Day 1 sources of funds include cash on hand plus expected loan repayments. The cumulative liquidity for Day 3 is negative, showing that Uri Bank should act now to raise an additional \$400,000 in cash before Day 3.

Critique of the Static Model

The static liquidity ladder provides a useful starting point for liquidity analysis. However, it is not designed for risk analysis. For example, if loans defaulted at a higher than expected rate, or depositors withdrew their funds, Uri Bank in the above example would have had a much worse liquidity outcome. By planning for the expected case, the bank exposes itself to the risk of liquidity shortfalls. Because of the high cost of those shortfalls, the bank needs to look at liquidity on a worst-case basis, not an expected basis.

To accomplish this, banks perform probabilistic analysis on their assets and liabilities to determine the likely and worst case cash requirements. Banks do not necessarily hold enough cash to cover their worst possible liquidity outcomes, but they should have credit lines large enough to cover the contingency of higher than expected liquidity demands.

Like market and credit risk models, probabilistic models of liquidity need to consider the features of all the assets and liabilities, and understand how their liquidity requirements interact to determine liquidity requirements. This is the topic of the next section.

2.2.2 Probabilistic models

We begin by examining the complexity of a number of the assets and liabilities on the bank's balance sheet, and how they are modeled for liquidity reporting purposes. The goal of this section is to help the student understand not only how banks measure liquidity risks of different types of assets or liabilities, but also how those individual risk assessments are combined into an aggregate risk report.

Deposits

Demand deposits may theoretically be withdrawn at any instant, suggesting that deposits present a great liquidity risk. On the other hand, corporations and individuals who use demand deposit accounts (such as checking accounts) exhibit "sticky" behavior, meaning that because of the costs of switching, absent extreme events, banks can expect most retail deposits to stay in place in the short term. Additionally, long-term deposits of various formats are not withdrawn frequently and at their maturity are often rolled over. Collectively, these deposits together with some of the more permanent demand deposits are called core deposits and serve as chief funding source for the bank.

On an everyday basis, the liquidity trends are easy to predict. Rents and mortgages are typically paid at the beginning of each month, which requires the depositors to have money available to make these withdrawals. Around holiday-time, chiefly around Christmas, large funds can be withdrawn to make end-of-year purchases. Withdrawals usually increase on Fridays before the weekend, and deposits increase on Mondays as shops and other businesses deposit the weekend's takings.

Sophisticated longer-term models of deposit retention incorporate historical behavior of different account types with macroeconomic overlays to reflect overall economic conditions such as changes in interest rates and unemployment. Regional banks are also sensitive to the economics of their regions. The balance between time deposits (such as CDs) and demand deposits can also be modeled, and the relationship tends to depend on the same sorts of variables.

The results of these models include short and long-term deposit level projections along with estimates in the volatility of deposits. These statistics are then used in the portfolio liquidity model to determine the risk attributable to depositor behavior.

Loans

In the case of loans, two types of liquidity demands arise. One has to do with the demand for loans, that is, new loans that must be funded. The other has to do with defaulting loans, where cash shortfalls can result.

Loan funding liquidity shortfalls can be managed by increasing sources of lending capital or by tightening underwriting requirements to reduce the number of loans funded. However, the latter option reduces profitability and jeopardizes relationships with good borrowers.

Default risk is measured and modeled comprehensively in major banks, and the expected time pattern of default is used to predict liquidity demands. When borrowers default, they put liquidity strains on banks.

Cash and Securities

Cash and liquid securities held as assets usually don't create liquidity risk directly, with the exception being margin calls on leveraged security investments (see the LTCM example above). However, since cash and securities are held as liquidity buffers, it is important to run risk models for the value of cash assets and securities to determine if they will be sufficient for meeting liquidity needs

Liquidity models for cash and securities can be derived from value-at-risk models, which were discussed in Chapter 5 of the Market Risk Management book in *the GARP Risk Series*. The VaR model computes the expected worst case value for the liquid portfolio with some confidence using historical data. In addition to a basic VaR model, risk models for these instruments should include the correlations to interest rates and other macroeconomic factors so that the model results can be integrated with liquidity risks of other assets and liabilities.

EXAMPLE

Many banks have counterparty trading agreements that call for same-day settlement of mark-to-market variations in their trade values. In this case, a bank could use its value-at-risk model to determine the likely worst case cash outlay on a given day to any or all of its bank counterparts.

Aggregation

The best liquidity risk models derive liquidity risks for each asset and liability based on common risk drivers. When risks are aggregated in these types of models, it is clear how aggregate interest rates, default rates, and other macroeconomic influences drive the need for additional liquidity.

For example, a downturn in the stock market may simultaneously increase consumers' cash needs and their propensity to default on credit cards. The bank's assets would fall in value, perhaps triggering collateral requirements on loans used to purchase the assets. Finally, if the bank's credit rating fell, its trading counterparts would require additional capital as well.

Given the difficulty of quantifying all these individual effects and cross effects, many banks will conduct stress tests on their liquidity ladders to assess the adequacy of their liquid assets to cover liabilities coming due. Here is one example from the Risk Institute.[6] In this example, the Day 1 liquidity ladder is shown under normal business conditions, under an institution-specific crisis, and under a general market crisis.

Table 5: Day 1 of the Maturity Ladder Under Alternative Scenarios (USD millions)

Day 1 of the maturity ladder under alternative scenarios (USD millions)

Cash inflows	**Normal business conditions (1)**	**Institution-specific crisis (3)**	**General market crisis (2)**
Maturing assets	100	100	90
Interest receivable	20	20	10
Asset sales	50	60	0
Drawdowns	10	0	5
Total	**180**	**180**	**105**
Cash outflows			
Maturing liabilities	50	50	50
Interest payable	10	10	10
Deposit runoffs	30	100	60
Drawdowns on lending commitments	50	60	75
Total	**140**	**220**	**195**
Liquidity Excess/(Shortfall)	**40**	**-40**	**-90**

A report like this one is meant to be used to determine whether a bank has sufficient liquid resources to withstand any reasonable liquidity crisis.

2.3 LIQUIDITY RISK MANAGEMENT

Liquidity risk models are only the beginning. Liquidity risk management generally requires a detailed contingency plan with both contracted and uncontracted liquidity provision. Contracted liquidity includes changing asset and liability structures to ensure liquidity is available when needed. It also includes credit lines set up by the bank to cover surprise liquidity requirements. Uncontracted provisions include contingency plans developed by the bank to address liquidity shortfalls.

It is important for a bank to plan for liquidity before it gets into financial distress — post hoc liquidity can be very expensive. An example of this was seen when Warren Buffett invested in Goldman Sachs' emergency preferred share issuance.

Under normal circumstances, liquidity can be adequately managed by shifting assets and liabilities, obtaining interbank loans, and drawing down credit lines. Under stress conditions, a bank must think aggressively about how it might increase liquidity.

The most common methods to increase liquidity in stress conditions include:

- Security issuance
- Interbank or government loans
- Obtaining additional credit lines
- Selling or securitizing assets

EXAMPLE

In the 2007 Annual Report, JPMChase reports that they issued $95.1 billion in long-term debt and trust preferred capital debt securities, explicitly not for funding or capital management purposes. In retrospect, this aided their liquidity position tremendously, since these steps were taken before the market collapsed completely in 2008.

The cash proceeds of these types of offerings increase bank liquidity unless the cash is invested in less liquid assets.

The first three methods of providing liquidity have already been covered. For example, we saw how Goldman Sachs and JPM Chase issued securities as a liquidity management measure. Less attention has been paid to securitization as a way to mitigate liquidity risk, so we will discuss securitization as an alternative to asset sales briefly.

2.3.1 Securitization

Securitization is a method by which banks sell illiquid assets. Technically, securitization of bank assets is the process by which banks — through various intermittent legal entities — issue bonds where:

- The payment of interest and repayment of principal on the bonds depends on the cash flow generated by a 'pool' of bank assets, and
- The bank has transferred its legal rights to payment of interest and repayment of principal to the bondholders.

When banks create such bond issues they greatly increase the inherent (endogenous) liquidity of the assets that have been securitized. In the absence of securitization a bank could only make the assets liquid by selling them, a process that is likely to be time consuming, expensive and require substantial effort.

EXAMPLE

A bank that has a large number of auto loans would find it prohibitively costly to sell the loans individually to raise cash. However, if the bank packages the auto loans into a securitized vehicle, obtains a credit rating and sells the low risk portion of the portfolio, it effectively turns illiquid loans into a security that can be sold, whether the bank decides to sell the security or not.

In the US, it is common for banks to securitize many of their retail loan assets — mortgages and revolving credit card debt — on a continuous basis and then hold the assets in securitized form. This removes these loans from the bank's balance sheet by selling them into a specially created entity often called special purpose entity or SPV. Through this transaction, the credit risk of these loans is moved into the SPV and as the SPV issues bonds to finance this purchase, the credit risk is ultimately moved to the holders of bonds the SPV issued.[7] This process makes the retail assets highly liquid and makes a bank's balance sheet easier to manage because:

- Any lack of capital (for example, due to rapid asset growth or as a consequence of bad debt growth) can be accommodated by selling the securitization bonds
- Any need to diversify credit risk can be accommodated by selling the bank's own securitized bonds (which may be naturally concentrated in a certain geographical location), and buying other bonds which increase diversification
- Any need for cash liquidity can be accommodated by securitizing assets through various bonds. Since these bonds do not depend on the credit standing of the bank for their value, they are not likely to be affected by any change in depositor or market sentiment towards the bank.

2.3.2 Broader Management Principles Around Liquidity Risk

Partly in response to the financial crisis, and partly continuing their tradition of advising banks on best liquidity risk management practices, the Bank for International Settlements published **Principles for Sound Liquidity Risk Management and Supervision** in June 2008.

"The principles underscore the importance of establishing a robust liquidity risk management framework that is well integrated into the bank-wide risk management process. The primary objective of this guidance is to raise banks' resilience to liquidity stress. Among other things, the principles seek to raise standards in the following areas:

- Governance and the articulation of a firm-wide liquidity risk tolerance;
- Liquidity risk measurement, including the capture of off-balance sheet exposures, securitisation activities, and other contingent liquidity risks that were not well managed during the financial market turmoil;

- Aligning the risk-taking incentives of individual business units with the liquidity risk exposures their activities create for the bank;
- Stress tests that cover a variety of institution-specific and market-wide scenarios, with a link to the development of effective contingency funding plans;
- Strong management of intraday liquidity risks and collateral positions;
- Maintenance of a robust cushion of unencumbered, high quality liquid assets to be in a position to survive protracted periods of liquidity stress; and
- Regular public disclosures, both quantitative and qualitative, of a bank's liquidity risk profile and management.

The principles also strengthen expectations about the role of supervisors, including the need to intervene in a timely manner to address deficiencies and the importance of communication with other supervisors and public authorities, both within and across national borders."

Many of these issues have been addressed in prior sections, so we will touch only on the unique points.

Firm-wide Liquidity Risk Tolerance

By setting a policy in advance and at the aggregate level, bank managers design a target maximum exposure to liquidity demands. Once the aggregate maximum is set and the calculations of liquidity risk are completed, banks can determine if corrective action is required.

Align Risk-Taking Incentives

A risk-taking department that has free rein to take liquidity risk will certainly squander it. To ensure that the bank's capacity for taking liquidity risk is not compromised by a single department, the bank must place a cost on the risk, i.e. penalize the business for taking excessive liquidity risk, and measure the performance of the business after computing the cost of its liquidity risk positions.

Stress Tests

While market-risk tests of liquidity are fairly commonplace, it is necessary for banks to also run their stress tests on liquidity scenarios. These stress tests combine market events (e.g. falling interest rates) with credit events (increasing defaults) and bank-specific events (declining credit rating triggering collateral calls). The stress tests must be designed to capture a wide range of realistic, unlikely yet possible outcomes.

Regular Public Reporting and Disclosures

It is in the bank's interest to inform its stakeholders how well liquidity is managed. Customers, debtholders and equityholders all prefer that a bank does not get into financial distress, and clearly the leading cause of bank distress is liquidity risk.

2.4 RISK REPORTING

Based on its experience with banks during the credit crisis, the FDIC, one of the main US banking regulators, has suggested[8] that banks should also create risk reports for their liquidity that address the following potential risk areas. These reports should be produced in addition to the usual probabilistic analysis and stress tests.

- Cash flow gaps
- Asset and funding concentration
- Critical assumptions used in credit projections
- Key early warning or risk indicators
- Funding availability
- Status of contingent funding sources
- Collateral uses

JPMChase discussed liquidity risk management extensively in their 2007 Annual Report (pp 70-72). The major headings include governance, funding, and credit ratings.

Governance

JPM's liquidity risk management is centralized in the treasury function. The ALCO (asset-liability committee) is responsible for the execution of the liquidity policy and the contingency funding plan. In sum, the groups' responsibility is to measure, monitor, report and manage liquidity risk.

> *"Treasury models historical liquidity trends, tracks historical and prospective on- and off-balance sheet liquidity obligations, identifies and measures internal and external liquidity warning measures to permit early detection of liquidity issues, and manages contingency planning (including identification and testing of various company-specific and market-driven stress scenarios). Various tools, which together contribute to an overall liquidity perspective, are used to monitor and manage liquidity. These include analysis of the timing of liquidity sources vs liquidity uses (i.e. funding gaps) over periods ranging from overnight to one year; management of debt and capital issuance to ensure that the illiquid portion of the balance sheet can be funded by equity, long-term debt, trust-preferred debt securities and deposits the Firm believes to be stable; and assessment of the Firm's capacity to raise incremental unsecured and secured funding."*

Funding

> *"Diversification of funding is an important component of the Firm's liquidity management strategy."*

Sources of funds include the stable portion of deposits, the stable portion of liability balances, and a variety of short and long-term instruments. The latter category includes purchased federal funds, commercial paper, bank notes, long-term debt and trust-preferred capital debt securities.

Flexibility in funding is afforded by JPMChase's reserves of unencumbered and liquid securities. These securities can be loaned in the repo market or sold in the asset securitization markets.

Credit Ratings

Credit rating changes can have an enormous impact on liquidity, but for JPMChase in 2007, the sensitivity to ratings changes was relatively low.

> *"The cost and availability of unsecured financing are influenced by credit ratings. A reduction in these ratings could have an adverse effect on the Firm's access to liquidity sources, increase the cost of funds, trigger additional collateral requirements and decrease the number of investors and counterparties willing to lend. Key factors in maintaining high credit ratings include a stable and diverse earnings stream, leading market positions, strong capital ratios, strong credit quality and risk management controls, diverse funding sources and disciplined liquidity monitoring procedures."*

2.5 CONCLUSIONS

Liquidity risk management during normal times can be as simple as cash management. In periods of high volatility and uncertain credit, liquidity issues become paramount to a bank, since they threaten the bank's health and even its existence. Whereas banks use liquidity ladders to understand their static liquidity position, probabilistic models are needed to understand the behavior of complex assets and liabilities, and their effect on a bank's liquidity. Also, stress testing can be done on these models to determine a bank's maximum likely liquidity requirement.

Liquidity can be supplied by the bank itself (selling assets), by the strength of the bank's balance sheet (borrowings), or by external parties. The bank's liquidity position, both sources and uses of cash, is usually managed as part of the asset and liability management function of the bank.

2.6 SUMMARY

Introduction to Liquidity Risk

- Interest rate risk in the banking book is the risk of loss due to adverse changes in interest rates.
- Liquidity risk in the banking book is the risk of not being able to fund the holding of an asset or the retirement of a liability.
- Liquidity risk management is a vital area of risk control.
- Historically, liquidity management had to do with estimating depositor behavior and drawdowns on credit lines.

- Nowadays, liquidity can be stressed by leveraged lending (if asset values fall), margin requirements and counterparty defaults.
- Banks address their needs with their endogenous, exogenous and external liquidity.
- Endogenous liquidity is the liquidity inherent in bank assets themselves.
- Exogenous liquidity (often called funding liquidity) is the liquidity provided to the bank by its liability structure, including its ability to borrow and obtain contingent lines.
- External liquidity is the noncontractual contingent capital supplied by investors and other institutions to support a bank during times of liquidity stress
- Liquidity mismatches can cause serious problems as was highlighted by the crisis at Long-Term Capital Management (LTCM), a US hedge fund.
- As a direct result of the LTCM crisis many trading businesses now ensure that they have better access to long-term funding through instruments such as committed funding lines (i.e., commercial bank commitments to lend to them).

Liquidity Risk Measurement

- The classical tool for measuring the bank's liquidity position is the liquidity ladder, a snapshot of the bank's projected cash flow sources and uses.
- The liquidity ladder is usually produced to assess short-term liquidity requirements.
- Gaps in liquidity can be filled by selling assets, drawing down credit lines, or issuing securities.
- The biggest problem with the liquidity ladder approach is that it does not address the probabilistic nature of cash flow requirements.
- No one can predict runs on the bank or customer demands for cash on their credit lines with certainty.
- Hence the best models consider the range of possible outcomes for liquidity demand, and the drivers of those outcomes.
- Liquidity models have the same level of complexity as VaR models and credit models, and the same shortfalls, such as reliance on past relationships and problems integrating risks across related assets.

Liquidity Risk Management

- Under normal circumstances, liquidity risk is well-behaved and relatively easy to manage.
- During times of stress, banks turn to security issuance, interbank or government loans, obtaining additional credit lines and selling or securitizing assets.
- As an example of security issuance, Goldman Sachs issued $5 billion in preferred stocks to Warren Buffett in order to help the company improve its liquidity position.

- Securitization of bank assets is the process by which banks issue bonds where the payment of interest and repayment of principal on the bonds depends on the cash flow generated by a 'pool' of bank assets, and the bank has transferred its legal rights to payment of interest and repayment of principal to the bondholders.
- When banks create such bond issues they greatly increase the inherent (endogenous) liquidity of the assets that have been securitized.
- In the US it is common for banks to securitize many of their retail assets on a continuous basis and then hold the assets in securitized form.

Risk Reporting

- Banks at a minimum should prepare liquidity ladders, probabilistic analysis and stress tests of their liquidity requirements.
- In addition, the FDIC recommends reports related to cash flow gaps, asset and funding concentration, critical assumptions used in credit projections, key early warning or risk indicators, funding availability, status of contingent funding sources and collateral uses.
- Excerpts of JPMChase's 2007 liquidity risk reporting are provided in the chapter.

Chapter 3

Bank Capital Management

This capstone chapter explains how the concepts of risk studied in the earlier chapters drive capital management decisions for banks. For banks, risk is a better measure of required capital than capital itself; models that estimate risk form the foundation for assessments of capital adequacy both for individual banks and the entire financial system.

This chapter reviews, sharpens and builds prior descriptions of capital and its components: the different types of capital, how capital is computed, managed, and increased or decreased. But a bank does not calculate capital in order to satisfy its regulators or for its own sake. The ultimate purpose of understanding capital is to optimize return on capital (RAROC, or risk-adjusted return on capital) for different activities and make financial decisions that maximize bank shareholder value relative to risk taken.

While every student of banking should understand regulatory capital, the focus of this volume has been on the economics of risk management and not on the regulation of risk management. However, because regulatory capital restricts the actions of banks, it is critical to consider from an economic perspective as well.

On completion of this chapter the reader will have a basic understanding of:

- The types of capital
- Regulatory and economic capital
- The components of Tier 1, Tier 2 and Tier 3 capital
- Capital deductions
- The ratios between different capital components
- The capital creation process
- The relationship between capital and risk measures
- Return and risk for economic capital (RAROC)
- Risk-based performance measurement at the bank level
- The importance of a culture of risk management

The final point may be the most important. If risk is the measure of capital for a bank, then bank managers must strive to maximize risk awareness and develop consistent standards for taking and avoiding risk. A common language — for risks, measures of risk, and return on risk — facilitates the development of the risk management culture.

3.1 TYPES OF CAPITAL

The management of a bank differs from the management of non-financial corporations. One important difference is that banks, unrestrained, might have incentives to increase their risks as much as possible. Suppose for example that a bank had $100 mm in capital but borrowed $100 billion to lend. If very few loans defaulted, the bank could profit enormously. Conversely, if there were larger than expected defaults, the bank would not lose more than $100 mm. Without regulation, the incentive to take excess risk would exist. Even though depositors might be protected by agencies such as the FDIC, the financial system would not be protected against excessive risk-taking by financial institutions collectively.

As another example of the difference between banks and non-financial corporations, consider the objectives of the two different corporation types. While a non-financial corporation may strive to maximize return on capital, a banker may not even know exactly how to measure capital. For example, if the bank enters into a number of futures trades, how should it compute the capital, particularly if no cash is put on margin to guarantee the trades? Or if the margin is in the form of interest-bearing securities?

As a third example, consider a bank that has issued debt. Debt puts cash into the bank, but at the same time, repayment provisions can jeopardize the sufficiency of the capital base. Should the debt be counted as part of the capital of the bank? Or, should it be given partial capital treatment to recognize the capital contribution on the one hand, but the obligation to repay on the other? The answer is not obvious.

Because international governments have an interest in preserving the integrity of the international banking system, they have passed regulations requiring minimum capital levels at banks. This requires that they define capital requirements reasonably, determine how capital is measured, and determine the appropriate forms of eligible capital for banks. Too much capital means banks can be inefficient and uncompetitive. Too little capital jeopardizes the health of the financial system.

3.1.1 Economic and Regulatory Capital

In non-financial firms, **capital** is the amount of funds and assets required to establish and run a business. Typically, capital is equity capital, the investment made by the owners in the firm as paid-in capital, which can be made through a cash infusion or a security issuance. Long-term borrowings can also be considered as capital, but not as equity capital. While companies generally try to maximize their return on invested capital, they usually take capital to be equal to the total amount of paid-in capital, or at least the amount of paid-in equity. Banks, however, due to significantly higher leverage may lose much more than the paid-in capital — their possible losses may exceed the amount of capital contributed from all their capital sources. Their possible losses, their capital at risk, or the level of losses the bank feels comfortable with, i.e. their **risk capital**, may exceed paid-in capital. This is exactly what regulators hope to avoid, since unexpected loss events could cause the failure of not just one bank, but many banks simultaneously.

If banks were unregulated, they would devise their own capital measures and make decisions to optimize their return on capital. The type of internal capital calculation they would use is known as **economic capital** (also risk capital), since it reflects the economic tradeoffs of the bank as accurately as the bank can represent them. The capital measures defined by regulators are known as regulatory capital. As a general rule, economic capital is determined by internal risk models, whereas **regulatory capital** is determined by rules imposed by an outside authority.

Advantages of Economic Capital

As a measure of capital, economic capital is generally believed to be a better measure of capital for a bank than regulatory capital, because economic capital reflects the possible losses the bank can bear based on the bank's own estimates of the risks it is taking, while regulatory — minimum — capital reflects the lowest level of capital the bank should have to meet the regulatory requirement. Arguably, banks are in a better position to understand their risks, and are motivated to understand them better than anyone else, so regulators expect bankers to have a more subtle and complete understanding of their capital. Since banks are putting their money at risk based on the capital calculations, they will do their best to ensure the calculations are accurate at the appropriate level of commercial standard.

Disadvantages of Economic Capital

Since the models for economic capital are derived by the banks themselves, regulators may be concerned that the models may be insufficient, unused, subject to significant model risk, or even manipulated. For these reasons, regulators would not likely accept capital constraints for banks linked purely to internal economic capital models.

Benefits of Regulatory Capital

From a regulatory perspective, internal models of economic capital are problematic since every bank uses a different model. If the banks use different models, it is difficult for a regulator to determine which banks are relatively well-capitalized or poorly capitalized relative to their business activities. For this reason, regulatory standards impose formulaic capital calculations for all of a bank's activities. In addition to the benefit of capital comparability across banks, regulatory calculations can help ensure that (a) banks are not missing key risks in their models and (b) banks are not using the capital calculations in any obvious way to "game" the banking regulation system.

Disadvantages of Regulatory Capital

By requiring formulaic interpretations of capital, regulatory models tend to overstate economic risk. For example, in early regulatory frameworks, all corporate debt was deemed to have the same risk level. While this helped regulators quickly compare risks across banks, it caused banks to shift to riskier corporate debts, since the returns were higher and the regulatory capital was the same. These types of activities became known as **regulatory capital arbitrage.**

3.1.2 Balancing Economic and Regulatory Capital

Which capital measure should a bank use for its internal decision-making? If a bank has confidence in its economic capital model, it will use that model for decision-making, but recognize that it has constraints on regulatory capital. This implies that while regulatory capital is an important guide for banks, it does not govern how they allocate their capital, except in cases where the regulatory capital calculations are much higher than economic capital. In these cases, it may be more important to focus on regulatory capital as a guide to their decision-making.

Looking at regulatory capital limits as a constraint on economic capital allocation, a bank's objective is to maximize its return on economic capital, after adjusting for the cost of excessive regulatory capital constraints. The most popular measure of economic capital is RAROC, the risk-adjusted return on capital, which is discussed at length later in this chapter. For now, we focus on the components of capital and the key issues of regulatory capital so the student can best understand the relationships between them.

3.1.3 JPMChase's Economic Risk Capital

Table 1: JPM Chase's Economic Risk Capital

JPMorgan Chase assesses its capital adequacy relative to the risks underlying the Firm's business activities, utilizing internal risk-assessment methodologies. The Firm measures economic capital primarily based upon four risk factors: credit risk, market risk, operational risk and private equity risk, principally for the Firm's private equity business.

Economic risk capital	**Yearly Average**	
(in billions)	**2007**	**2006**
Credit risk[(a)]	**$30.0**	$26.7
Market risk	**9.5**	9.9
Operational risk	**5.6**	5.7
Private equity risk	**3.7**	3.4
Economic risk capital	**48.8**	45.7
Goodwill	**45.2**	43.9
Other[(b)]	**24.7**	21.1
Total common stockholders' equity	**$118.7**	$110.7

(a) Incorporates a change to the wholesale credit risk methodology, which has been modified to include a through-the-cycle adjustment (described below). The prior period has been revised to reflect this methodology change.
(b) Reflects additional capital required, in management's view, to meet its regulatory and debt rating objectives.

JPM's report of economic risk capital demonstrates the link between risk capital and equity. While economic risk capital including market, credit, operational and private equity risk totals $49 billion, the calculation of equity capital shows what adjustments are made. Arguably, the goodwill adjustment is an accounting adjustment (with limited risk or economic significance) that can be considered part of the overall $70 billion adjustment to get from $49 billion in risk capital to $119 billion in equity.

In theory, if the economic capital calculation were sufficient, JPM would not need more than $49 billion in equity. In this case, JPM could buy back $70 billion of its equity. Yet, footnote "b" explains that additional capital is "required, in management's view, to meet its regulatory and debt rating objectives." This makes it clear that (a) regulatory capital exceeds economic capital and (b) JPM values a high credit rating, one that provides comfort to customers and counterparties of the bank and thereby increases its business volume.

3.2 COMPUTING ECONOMIC CAPITAL

Economic capital is a measure of a bank's capital requirement that relates directly to the aggregate risk the bank is running, in effect meeting unexpected losses in excess of expected losses. To survive in the long term a bank needs to overcome periods during which extreme circumstances could cause it to sustain large losses. If the bank has capital levels to support it through such times it will survive; if it does not it will fail.

3.2.1 Economic Capital and Value at Risk (VaR)

The use of economic capital as a measure of risk stems directly from the development of Value at Risk (VaR) methodology which took place in the trading businesses of banks. The VaR methodology provided a successful tool for both supervisors and bank management.

The response to the question can be found in the bank's risk report, which may typically contain a statement similar to: "The trading portfolio has a daily VaR of USD 5 million at the 99% confidence level." In this statement the confidence level relates to a level of probability that some event will occur, i.e. in simple terms the VaR expressed above says that within the period of one trading day there is a 1% (100%-99%) chance that losses on the trading portfolio could exceed USD 5 million.

This may seem a low probability; however, looked at another way, it says that the bank would not lose more than USD 5 million in trading on more than 2 1/2 days in a year. This assumes that there are approximately 250 days a year when the markets are open for trading. In practice 21/2 days would be rounded up to three days as profit and loss is calculated daily. Two and half days is an approximation and depends on a number of factors, such as the accuracy of the model. Notwithstanding these and other shortcomings, this calculation and the value it yields gives a very clear insight into measuring risk levels in different portfolios and in different banks. VaR thus represents a major step forward for both management and supervisors trying to understand the risks a bank was running in its trading businesses.

A bank with a higher VaR is running a higher level of risk. For instance, Bank G has a VaR of USD 10 million at the 99% confidence level while Bank H has a VaR of USD 5 million at the same confidence level. Bank G is running twice the risk of Bank H, as measured by VaR. Inevitably the use of VaR led the senior management of banks to ask a further question: "So how bad could the bank's losses be in those 2 1/2 days?"

And the response to this question depends on the risk the bank is taking, and is answered by calculation of economic capital.

3.2.2 Economic Capital Methodology

The answer is not as simple as it is with VaR as it depends on two complicating factors. First, the losses are typically unexpected and unlikely, and the more unlikely the event, the less data there is to support any analysis. Second, a combination of poor data and a need to predict very infrequent events requires more complex statistical modeling techniques, which are inherently prone to errors and simplifications.

VaR gives no indication of the actual losses that will occur beyond the 99% confidence level on a daily basis. Bank G is running twice the VaR, and hence the risk, of Bank H. However, it does not automatically follow that Bank G will lose twice as much as Bank H when losses exceed the 99% confidence level. Bank G's losses may be less, the same, or more than twice those of Bank H, because the losses beyond the 99% confidence level could differ significantly for each bank, and may not be known prior to the estimation of risk or economic capital.

It will also be evident that for many banks it is important that the answer to the 'extent of losses' question should cover all the risks the bank was running, including credit, operational, and other risks, not just those risks that stem from its trading portfolio. For many commercial banks this also means measuring potential losses from corporate and/or retail loans, as these credit risks are often the largest source of potential loss. In addition, it means considering other risks such as those being run through their operations areas, (i.e. operational risk).

The most sophisticated banks soon developed models that measured the potential extreme and unexpected losses in scenarios that involved losses from a combination of their market risk (including that held in the banking book — see Chapter 1), credit risk, operational risk and other risks.

These models then estimated the capital necessary for the bank to survive 'worst case' losses from a combination of these risk areas.

3.2.3 Problems with Measuring Economic Capital

The diagram below is commonly used to highlight a number of the issues in understanding economic capital models.

Figure 1: Problems with Underlying Economic Capital

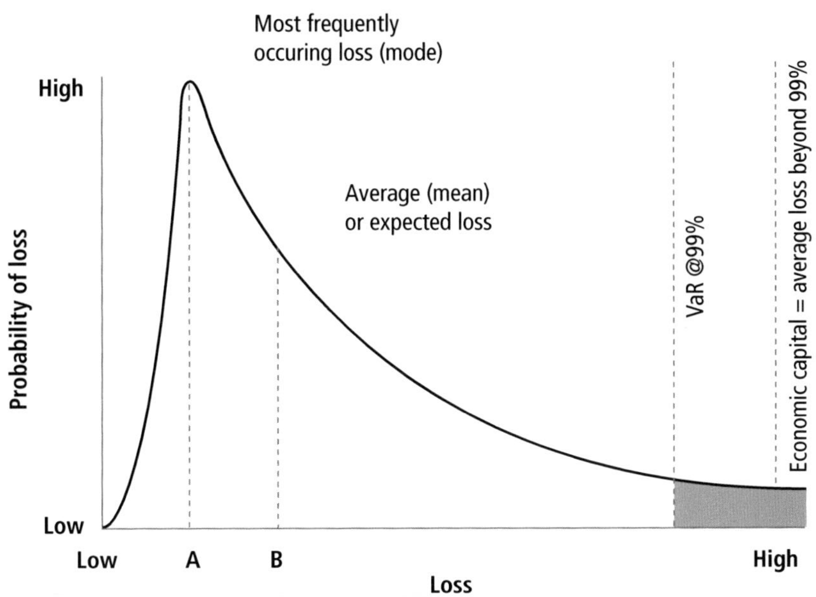

The diagram above illustrates several important points:

- It represents (an assumed) statistical distribution of the potential losses a bank might sustain over a future time period, for example one year
- It is 'skewed,' i.e. the range of possible losses above the average (mean) is much greater than those below the average
- The loss that is most likely to occur (the mode) is below the average (mean) loss

- The economic capital will be required to cover a larger loss and will therefore be higher than the capital needed to cover the 99% confidence interval as commonly used for VaR calculations. In many cases, the economic capital level is taken to be the probability-weighted average of all losses beyond the 99% confidence level, as shown in the figure.

Important conclusions can be drawn from the diagram. These are:

- In most years the bank would look more profitable than it will be 'on average' as its most likely loss (A) is below the level of the average (B)
- When loss levels are high they are really high, i.e. bad years don't come along very often but when they do, beware!
- A sufficiently well capitalized bank (i.e., one capitalized to survive bad years) will look over-capitalized most of the time, in the sense that most of its capital will appear to have been unused.

The explanation for the above conclusions is relatively simple to understand in that:

- Losses for most commercial banks are dominated by credit losses and occur in large amounts only when the whole economy goes into recession, and the bank suffers losses in its corporate and retail lending books at the same time. (Few banks have broad geographical diversification of their business across many economies.)
- Many commercial banks have high concentrations of risk, both for geographical as well as historical reasons. A bank could have strong relationships in a certain part of the country or with a particular industry. For example many banks with origins as mortgage lenders are very reliant on the economic prospects of the housing market.

It is the insight these models give to portfolio concentration risks that is of particular interest to supervisors. In fact many supervisors have expressed concern that Basel II based credit grading models do not provide adequate information in the area of concentration risk management.

3.2.4 Model Problems — Data

The data available to 'populate' and therefore measure such distributions of losses are difficult to assemble. There are a number of reasons for this; chief amongst them is that they require the bringing together of significantly different measures of risk.

Losses from trading can be easily updated on a daily basis and there are thousands of transactions a day, of which a significant number are likely to produce losses. As a result a year of daily data will provide a good history from which a VaR model for market risk is derived.

In contrast, the transactions on which credit losses are based are undertaken much less often than trading transactions. They also last much longer which means losses are less frequently observed. For these reasons credit losses are usually assessed using annual loss data on losses. It should be noted that if historical data were used the model would require 100 years of back data to establish the loss at 99%! For this reason other techniques have to be used.

It is difficult to populate operational risks models with data especially since some operational risks are difficult to quantify in financial loss terms. In practice the capital requirements are usually assessed over an annual period as they are for credit risk. However, as with credit risk the difficulty of assembling sufficient historical data means that other statistical measurement techniques are commonly used.

3.2.5 Adding Up Economic Capital

The different categories of risk under Basel II, market, credit and operational risk, all share a common development. For each category of risk, a computation similar to the one shown in Figure 1 is performed. In each case, the measure of capital is the difference between a measure of the maximum loss and the expected loss. While the concept is called "VaR" for market risk or "unexpected loss" for credit risk, the result is the same.

Since the capital is diversified across market, credit and operational risk, bankers may ask why the aggregate capital is computed as the sum of the three capital measures, instead of a sum adjusted for a diversification benefit. In theory, the risk of the sum should be less than the sum of the risks.

In practice, it would be very difficult for banks to estimate the correlations between the risk categories and therefore the diversification benefit. Regulators would not be able to assert a standard because the correlations would be different for banks with different activity levels. For example, the correlation between market capital and credit capital would be different for a bank that focuses on trading and one that focuses on lending.

Therefore, practitioners use the most conservative assumption possible, assume all risks are perfectly correlated, and simply add the risk measures.

3.2.6 Supervisory Acceptance of Economic Capital Models

Supervisors following the principles of the Basel II Accord, are tasked with an oversight responsibility of the various internal capital adequacy models estimating the economic capital of banks. In this capacity, supervisors need to ensure that the models comply with regulatory pronouncements, and address several concerns. These concerns stretch from data issues, such as the quality, relevance and adequacy of data available in the models and the input into these models to the relative newness of such models that make verification difficult. Additionally, there may be concerns related to timing differences. Operational risks and operational risk capital are often assessed on an annual basis as are credit risks and credit risk capital. But market risks are assessed on a more frequent basis and can focus on such short time periods as one day, a week, or 10 trading days. It is not only adding up the risks and the required risk capital across different time frequencies that causes problems — the potential correlation across these risks are difficult to quantify and are generally poorly understood.

The timing and measuring differences lead to final complexity where regulators and banks are trying to resolve. The various models ultimately support decisions on retaining capital. The methods of measuring very unlikely and infrequently occurring loss events can be difficult to understand. For example, how would a bank react if the likelihood of a certain level of extreme loss has risen from 0.05% (5 in 10,000) to 0.1% (1 in 1,000)? Differently put, how would the capital requirements change if the likelihood of a loss event occurring increases from occurring once every 40 years to once every 4 years? Should the bank raise more capital or ignore it?

A number of sophisticated banks do use economic capital models to support decisions regarding the level and structure of capital they believe they should hold. They are also used for pricing transactions against the likely level of loss the bank could sustain over time. Additionally, such models give valuable insight into a bank's portfolio concentration risk. Some major banks even publish the results from their economic capital models in their annual accounts attesting to their importance in helping management make decisions relating to capital and risk.

Given the widespread use of such models they clearly could not be ignored by supervisors. Under Pillar 2 of the Basel II Accord, banks using such models are expected to share and discuss their results with supervisors. There are also requirements for sophisticated banks to develop methodologies to look at capital in relation to their own risk estimates. Such methodologies may and often will involve the development and use of economic capital models.

3.3 COMPONENTS OF CAPITAL

While the provisions are voluntary, nearly every major jurisdiction has embraced the international standard, though jurisdictions have been free to choose certain parameters, such as the timing of the adoption of the capital rules. For students unfamiliar with Basel I and Basel II, a review of the FBR material is recommended.

This section covers the details about what is considered capital for the purposes of regulatory calculations.

3.3.1 Bank Capital

In the FBR, eligible capital was defined as shareholders' equity and bank-issued bonds structured in a way as to qualify as debt capital. Debt capital can best be defined as capital that will be repaid — should the bank go into liquidation — after depositors and other debt holders of the bank have been repaid, but before equity capital holders. For this reason it is known as subordinated debt (to the bank's depositors and other lenders to the bank). Equity capital constitutes fully paid ordinary shares/common stock and non-cumulative perpetual preferred shares/stock. The terms 'stocks' and 'shares' are, for the purposes of this chapter, interchangeable. Hereafter only shares will be used in the text.

The capital of a bank, subject to Basel regulation, can be described as having two major tiers: Tier 1 and Tier 2, plus one additional tier which has a very restricted use, Tier 3. A bank's capital structure becomes more complicated when considering how capital is created and the variety of debt and equity instruments which capital markets can originate.

3.3.2 Tier 1 Capital

The Basel Committee considers that the key element of capital on which supervisors should place the most emphasis is equity capital, to which should be added the accrual of profits to reserves. Together these two elements constitute core capital.

To this core capital a bank can add what is often called 'innovative' Tier 1 capital to create its total Tier 1 capital. Innovative Tier 1 structures are capital market instruments which 'sit' in terms of repayment between shareholders' equity and debt, and which have features of both. As these innovative capital products are subordinated to debt issued by the bank, they are typically structured as preferred stock. Supervisors place strict rules on the features of such market instruments and the extent to which they can be issued.

Tier 1 capital also includes certain disclosed reserves that the bank has. Disclosed reserves are typically those reserves that are created using the bank's after-tax income.

3.3.3 Tier 2 Capital

Tier 2 capital comprises debt capital that is subordinated (to the interests of depositors and other creditors) in the event of a bank going into liquidation, but is not subordinated to equity and innovative capital products that would count as Tier 1 capital. However, it excludes perpetual non-cumulative preference shares, which are typically used as one of the innovative capital products.

Additionally, Tier 2 capital can include undisclosed reserves, including the general reserves the bank may make against its expected loan losses.

The liquidation of any company usually results in not all of its creditors being repaid from the liquidation (sale) of the company's assets. The ranking of creditors for repayment on default (i.e., who gets paid first, second, etc.) thus matters greatly. While debt capital holders will be paid prior to shareholders, they will only be paid after depositors and other creditors. Therefore the holders of debt capital will be the last creditors to be paid following a liquidation (prior to any distribution to Tier 1 capital instrument holders). Shareholders as owners are not actually creditors of the company whose equity they own. Any residual value in a liquidation — following payments to all creditors — is the property of equity investors.

Banks often assign the components of their Tier 2 capital into an upper and lower Tier 2 capital. Upper Tier 2 capital is distinguished from other subordinated debt issues that pay interest (and where failure to do so would be an event of default). Upper Tier 2 capital comprises:

- Preference shares (technically a form of debt) that confer on issuers the right to defer payment of a fixed dividend. Because the dividend is a fixed percentage of the debt, in most circumstances it is similar in nature to an interest payment
- General provisions comprising provisions against loan losses which may reasonably be expected to happen (often taken within the next year), but which cannot be related to a specific default. It should be noted that the inclusion of general provisions is subject to a limit of 1.25% of risk-weighted assets under the Standardized Approach to credit risk. If expected loss (EL) is greater than the total provisions then 50% of the difference is deducted from each of Tier 1 and Tier 2 capital. If EL is less than the provisions the difference is reflected in Tier 2 capital
- Certain revaluation reserves, i.e. an increase in capital resulting from the revaluation of certain assets such as real estate also belong in this category of capital
- Certain hybrid debt capital instruments which are similar to equity and which must include the ability to support ongoing losses without triggering liquidation.

Lower Tier 2 capital includes subordinated debt issues that pay interest must also have a repayment date which must be at least five years on initial issue and of which only:

- 80% of outstanding debt can count as Tier 2 capital four years before repayment
- 60% in year 3
- 40% in year 2
- 20% in year 1.

3.3.4 Tier 3 Capital

Tier 3 capital is debt capital that can only be used to support market risk in the trading book of the bank. It comprises subordinated debt that is issued initially for a minimum of two years. In addition debt repayments must be suspended if the bank's capital falls below its individual capital ratio as set by its national supervisor.

3.3.5 Options on Capital Instruments

There are also restrictions on the attachment of options to all debt capital instruments used for capital purposes. If the purchaser has an option to demand repayment before the debt's scheduled repayment date (a 'put' option), the option date will count as the repayment date for capital purposes. If the issuer has the right to repay before the scheduled repayment date (a 'call' option), it will be ignored for capital purposes, unless the issuer is due to pay a higher rate of interest as compensation to the holder for not having exercised the option (known as a '**step up clause**').

3.3.6 Deductions from Capital

When calculating regulatory capital following the rules laid down in the Basel II framework, deductions are typically made for goodwill, investments made in subsidiaries, and the bank's equity holdings of other banks. Each of these topics is explored in sequence.

Goodwill deduction

Goodwill can often be seen as a capital item in company balance sheets. It arises as a result of the purchase of a business for more than the value of the capital of the acquired company as it is valued in that company's balance sheet. The excess payment to the shareholders of the acquired company becomes goodwill in the new consolidated balance sheet of the acquiring and acquired companies.

Under both Basel I and II, Tier 1 capital is subjected to a number of adjustments. One important adjustment is the deduction of any goodwill item in the balance sheet. The balance sheet of the new (acquired plus acquiring) bank will, depending on the size of the goodwill payment made to the acquired bank's shareholders, have less Tier 1 capital than that which the banks independently had before the acquisition. Since the purpose of acquisition is often to grow the business the reduced Tier 1 capital may well lead to the need to issue new shares.

Investments in subsidiaries

Investments in subsidiaries engaged in banking and similar activities, where the subsidiary is not consolidated into the regulated banking group's balance sheet, will result in a deduction from capital of the book value of the equity investment.

Holding of shares in another bank

In a number of countries it is common for a bank to have its capital reduced by the value of the shares it holds in other banks. This is subject to the discretion of the local supervisor.

3.3.7 Ratios Between Tiers of Capital

The Basel Committee sets out rules for the ratios that banks should maintain between different classes of equity. The primary restriction is that Tier 2 capital cannot exceed 50% of a bank's total regulatory capital. Furthermore, innovative instruments in Tier 1 are limited to a maximum of 15% of Tier 1 capital after deductions are made, and the lower Tier 2 capital, typically consisting of subordinated debt issues, may only equal up to 50% of core capital. Additionally local supervisors often impose a wider range of additional ratio requirements between different tiers and sub-tiers of capital.

3.3.8 The Capital Creation Process

Banks raise new equity capital for a variety of reasons and in a number of ways. The main reasons for raising a large amount of new capital are as a result of:

- The write-off of loans destroying existing capital and thus requiring new capital to support the bank's remaining business, or
- Senior management asking existing and potential shareholders to support a strategy of rapid growth in the balance sheet through either new business generation or a proposed acquisition.

3.3.9 Acquisitions and Capital

The reason banks often need to issue capital after making an acquisition is that the acquiring bank usually needs to pay a premium to the acquired bank. It should be noted that when the acquisition is being made the shareholders and markets will be more concerned with the premium to the current share price of the target bank. This premium should not be confused with the 'book value' of the shareholders' equity which is relevant to bank capital for regulatory purposes.

3.3.10 Capital and Profits

Banks that are profitable create a flow of new capital on a continuing basis, as profits after bad debt and other provisions are available for distribution to shareholders. It is usual however, especially for a bank whose business is growing, to retain some of the profits to add to its Tier 1 capital base. These retained profits are called 'retentions'. Retentions allow the bank to support new business without needing to ask shareholders for new capital. Raising capital through the shareholders is a process that if carried out on a regular basis is time-consuming and expensive.

The process of adding to a bank's Tier 1 capital through retentions is carried out on an annual basis when its shareholders approve the bank's audited report and accounts, as recommended by the bank's senior management. In practice one of the most important approvals that shareholders give is to the distribution of profits. The distribution can be divided between profits to be retained as new capital, and those returned to shareholders in the form of dividends.

While the reporting process is, by law, usually done on an annual or semi-annual basis (although quarterly reporting is the accepted practice in the US and is used by some companies in certain other jurisdictions) the process of profit creation is continuous. The Basel Committee recognizes this by allowing audited interim profits, net of any anticipated tax and dividends, to be included in Tier 1 capital subject to approval by the bank's auditors. This is particularly useful for banks with rapidly growing businesses and, consequently, a rapidly growing balance sheet. If they were forced to wait for a full year before retained profits became available as capital, banks might need to raise interim injections of capital from shareholders to maintain their business growth.

3.3.11 JPMChase's Regulatory Capital

Table 2: JPM Chase's Regulatory Capital

The Board of Governors of the Federal Reserve System (the "Federal Reserve Board") establishes capital requirements, including well-capitalized standards for the consolidated financial holding company. The Office of the Comptroller of the Currency establishes similar capital requirements and standards for the Firm's national banks, including JPMorgan Chase Bank, N.A., and Chase Bank USA, N.A.

JPMorgan Chase maintained a well-capitalized position, based upon Tier 1 and Total capital ratios at December 31, 2007 and 2006 as indicated in the tables below.

Capital ratios

December 31,	**2007**	2006	Well-capitalized ratios
Tier 1 capital ratio	**8.4%**	8.7%	6.0%
Total capital ratio	**12.6**	12.3	10.0
Tier 1 leverage ratio	**6.0**	6.2	NA
Total stockholders' equity to assets	**7.9**	8.6	NA

Risk-based capital components and assets

December 31, (in millions)	**2007**	2006
Total Tier 1 capital	**$88,746**	$81,055
Total Tier 2 capital	**43,496**	34,210
Total capital	**$132,242**	$115,265
Risk-weighted assets	**$1,051,879**	$935,909
Total adjusted average assets	**1,473,541**	1,308,699

Tier 1 capital was $88.7 billion at December 31, 2007, compared with $81.1 billion at December 31, 2006, an increase of $7.7 billion. The increase was due primarily to net income of $15.4 billion; net issuances of common stock under the Firm's employee stock-based compensation plans of $3.9 billion; net issuances of $2.0 billion of qualifying trust preferred capital debt securities; and the after-tax effects of the adoption of new accounting principles reflecting increases of $287 million for SFAS 157, $199 million for SFAS 159 and $436 million for FIN 48. These increases were partially offset by decreases in Stockholders' equity net of Accumulated other comprehensive income (loss) due to common stock repurchases of $8.2 billion and dividends declared of $5.2 billion. In addition, the change in capital reflects the exclusion of an $882 million (after-tax) valuation adjustment to certain liabilities pursuant to SFAS 157 to reflect the credit quality of the Firm. Additional information regarding the Firm's capital ratios and the federal regulatory capital standards to which it is subject is presented in Note 28 on pages 166–167 of this Annual Report.

The JPM report is particularly useful since it shows regulatory capital and compliance with all the relevant ratios discussed above. In addition, the discussion in the text below the table shows what management actions have affected the level of regulatory capital in the past year.

3.4 RISK AND RETURN FOR FINANCIAL INSTRUMENTS

In classical finance theory, corporations were advised to undertake business activities as long as the expected return exceeded the minimum return required by well-diversified shareholders. A well-diversified shareholder has its assets spread across a large group of different investments and would typically not suffer substantial losses if one or a few of the individual investments would fail. If corporations followed this advice blindly, they might find themselves taking unduly high risks, a situation that would be remedied by recapitalizing the corporation to absorb the increased risk. Failing to recapitalize, the corporation would increase its risk of bankruptcy.

Banks cannot afford to follow the classical finance advice, since they are required by regulation to maintain risk levels within their current capitalization. They must have enough equity to sustain losses at conservatively estimated levels. Because of this, every risky transaction the bank enters uses up some of the bank's limited risk capacity. In order to ensure that the limited risk capacity is used wisely, banks put a cost on risk. Each transaction must earn not only the minimum return required by shareholders, but an additional return due to the expense of risk.

3.4.1 Risk-Adjusted Return on Capital (RAROC) of a Single Transaction

The most widely used measure of the cost of risk is RAROC, or the Risk-Adjusted Return on Capital, first developed by Bankers Trust in the late 1970s. On a forward-looking basis, RAROC is defined to be the following ratio:

Forward-looking RAROC = [Expected Profit Net of All Financing Costs] / Value-at-Risk

At Bankers Trust in the 1990s, the VaR was computed at the 99% confidence level for one year, and a threshold RAROC of 25% was used. This implied that any deal done by the bank had to have an expected net profit that exceeded 25% of its VaR.

EXAMPLE

Bankers Trust has an opportunity to do a securitization deal for a credit card company, but has to retain a portion of the residual risk of the deal with an estimated VaR of $10 MM. Its fees for the deal are $3 MM, and the short-term financing costs are $600,000.

Profitability net of financing is $2.4 MM and the risk charges are $2.5 MM. The deal will have to be restructured in order to increase profitability or reduce the residual risk to an acceptable level. This could be accomplished by raising the fees, hedging the transaction or selling a portion of the residual risk to an outside buyer.

RAROC allows analysts to convert a measure of risk into a measure of cost and converts qualitative tradeoffs between return and risk into a quantitative tradeoff that can be rigorously enforced throughout a bank. By enforcing this discipline, the bank can ensure that each of its departments is considering the cost of risk in exactly the same way, and deciding how to structure and accept transactions within the same risk appetite guidelines.

Regulatory Capital Adjustment

Certain products might require a higher level of regulatory capital than expected relative to their risk. In these cases, projects must be subject to an incremental excess regulatory capital charge to ensure that projects do not foreclose other opportunities that use regulatory capital more efficiently. A surplus regulatory capital charge can be deducted from the numerator in the RAROC calculation.

VaR as a Measure of Capital

The RAROC equation in the last section may seem peculiar to analysts who would expect returns to be measured on the basis of cash investment. Indeed, the risks of many types of investments can be measured in this way. For example, an investor in a junk bond may expect to lose as much as his cash investment in the bond, but not more. However, bank transactions can be extremely complex, and require little to no cash. Despite requiring no cash, they have the potential to require additional cash in the future, unlike a junk bond investment. For this reason, it is more relevant to a bank to consider the range of possible future cash outlays associated with an investment rather than merely its initial cash outlay.

EXAMPLE

The bank takes a long position in the oil futures market that requires a 2% margin, i.e., the bank has to deposit 2% of the value of the contract with the broker. The futures contracts were priced at $60 per barrel (bbl) at inception, and rose by $3 to $63. The VaR on the position is estimated to be $10.

One would think that the return is 5%, or 3/60. However, the bank only paid 2% of $60 or $1.20 in margin per bbl. Alternatively, one would be tempted to think the return on investment is the return on the margin, which is 250%, or 3/1.20. This is also incorrect, since the bank could lose more than $1.20/bbl on the contract if the price declines.

The best answer is to determine the maximum likely future cash outlay — the reasonably expected loss on the position. This can be estimated by a VaR calculation. By linking VaR, the reasonably expected loss on the position to the realized profit, the risk and the returns are captured. Thus from a risk-adjusted return point of view RAROC is 30%, or 30% =3/10.

In summary, those who measure return on investment do so because cash is a scarce commodity and needs to be allocated wisely to those investments that provide the overall highest cash return. Those who measure return on risk (i.e. RAROC) do so because cash is relatively plentiful and risk is the scarce commodity. In many bank transactions, VaR is a better measure of capital than the initial cash outlay.

3.4.2 Combining Financial Instruments Into Portfolios

In the RAROC discussion above, we analyzed the case of a single bank transaction. In that example, the VaR of a stand-alone transaction was $10 MM. However, since the bank runs a large portfolio with a large number of transactions, the actual risk to the bank of the transaction is less than $10 MM. The reason for this is diversification. As a bank invests in transactions with different kinds of risks, it can expect to enjoy a diversification benefit from investing in new transactions. The lower the correlation, the greater the diversification benefit. If the correlation between a new transaction and the bank's portfolio is negative, the transaction is called a hedge of the bank's portfolio risks.

EXAMPLE

The bank's VaR is $100 MM prior to the transaction. If the new transaction correlates perfectly with the bank's current risks, there is no diversification benefit; the total VaR of the bank rises to $110 MM. If the correlation of the new transaction with the bank portfolio is zero, the incremental risk is negligible, only $0.5 MM. If the new transaction hedges the bank's current risk perfectly, at a correlation of -1, the bank risk with the transaction falls to $90 MM.

The chart below shows how the diversification benefit depends on the correlation between the new transaction and the existing bank portfolio; diversification benefits increase the lower the correlation.

Figure 2: Portfolio VaR with New Transaction

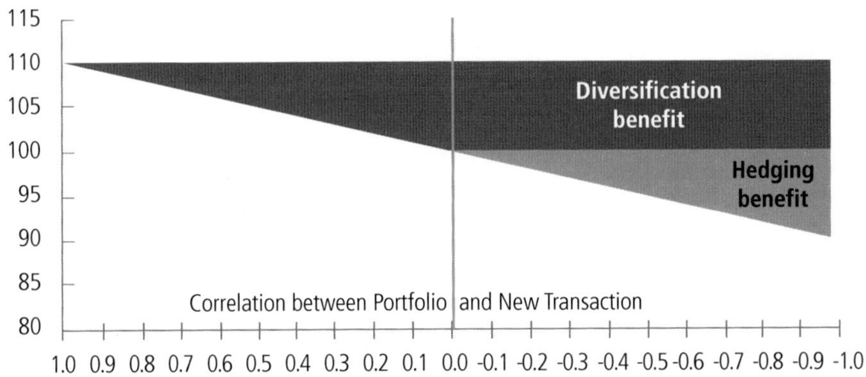

It should be noted that the relationship is not exactly linear, though the graph may suggest that in this instance, a straight line approximates the relationship. The exact formula is:

New Bank VaR = √[Bank VaR2 + Transaction VaR2 + 2 x correlation x Bank VaR x Transaction VaR]

If the correlation between the new transaction and the existing bank portfolio is 0.25, the new bank VaR is √(1002 + 102 + 2 x 0.25 x 100 x 10) = $102.96 MM.

In most banks, the diversification benefit is assumed to accrue to the bank, not to the transaction. One argument for this is that correlation is rarely certain, therefore the bank effectively assumes perfect correlation amongst its transactions in order to be conservative. In a crisis situation, such as the credit crisis of 2008-9, this may not have been a bad assumption, as seemingly unrelated markets all moved dramatically at the same time. A second reason for this assumption is that the bank can pass on some of its expected diversification benefit by reducing the cost of risk to its business units. This would imply, for example, that the bank may require an overall RAROC of 35%, but charges its business lines 25% knowing that it will achieve some diversification benefit.

3.4.3 Portfolio Return and Risk

Suppose a bank department wishes to know how portfolios of transactions affect its overall risk level. If every transaction has a profitability of $1 MM before risk charges, and a VaR of $10 MM, it would appear that each transaction by itself would not satisfy the bank's RAROC criteria. However, the story changes if the transactions are not perfectly correlated. In this case, the risk increases as more transactions are completed, but the risk rises more slowly than the profitability. The graph below illustrates how transaction volume increases RAROC through diversification. All transactions are assumed to be identically structured, with identical correlations.

Figure 3: Transaction Volume Impact on RAROC

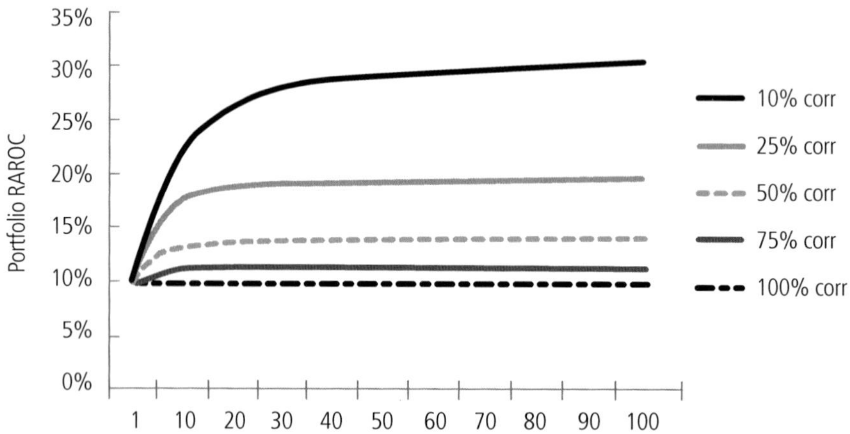

The maximum multiple of RAROC achievable is equal to the multiplicative inverse of the square root of the correlation. For example, if the transactions have a common correlation of 0.25, the maximum RAROC multiple is $1/\sqrt{0.25} = 2$. Raising the RAROC from 10% to 20% will still not meet the bank's criteria for profitability. In this case, with 25% correlation, each transaction must have an individual RAROC of 12.5% to meet a total department threshold of 25%, and the department must expect to do at least 100 transactions. Alternatively, the department would have to find other risk mitigating alternatives to make the department successful in RAROC terms.

In summary, portfolios of transactions will generally show a higher RAROC than the average of the transaction RAROCs. This is because even a small amount of diversification benefit allows the portfolio VaR to grow at a slower rate than portfolio profitability.

3.4.4 Estimates of JPMChases's RAROC

Given the development in the last two sections, it may seem reasonable to expand the RAROC framework to evaluate the performance of all the business units of a bank. We can see how this exact objective has been accomplished at JPMChase.

In its 2007 Annual Report, JPMChase states (p. 63):

"The firm's framework for allocating capital is based upon the following objectives:

- Integrate firmwide capital management activities with capital management activities within each of the lines of business
- Measure performance consistently across all lines of business; and
- Provide comparability with peer firms for each of the lines of business

Equity for a line of business represents the amount the Firm believes the business would require if it were operating independently, incorporating sufficient capital to address economic risk measures, regulatory capital requirements and capital levels for similarly rated peers."

Table 3: Line of Business Equity

The Firm's framework for allocating capital is based upon the following objectives:

- integrate firmwide capital management activities with capital management activities within each of the lines of business;
- measure performance consistently across all lines of business; and
- provide comparability with peer firms for each of the lines of business.

Equity for a line of business represents the amount the Firm believes the business would require if it were operating independently, incorporating sufficient capital to address economic risk measures, regulatory capital requirements and capital levels for similarly rated peers. Capital is also allocated to each line of business for, among other things, goodwill associated with such line of business' acquisitions since the Merger. In management's view, this methodology assigns responsibility to the lines of business to generate returns on the amount of capital supporting acquisition-related goodwill. At the time of the Merger, the Firm assigned to the Corporate segment an amount of equity capital equal to the then current book value of goodwill from and prior to the Merger. Return on equity is measured and internal targets for expected returns are established as a key measure of a business segment's performance. The Firm may revise its equity capital-allocation methodology again in the future.

In accordance with SFAS 142, the lines of business perform the required goodwill impairment testing. For a further discussion of goodwill and impairment testing, see Critical accounting estimates and Note 18 on pages 96–98 and 154–157, respectively, of this Annual Report.

Line of business equity	Yearly Average	
(in billions)	**2007**	2006
Investment Bank	**$21.0**	$20.8
Retail Financial Services	**16.0**	14.6
Card Services	**14.1**	14.1
Commercial Banking	**6.5**	5.7
Treasury & Securities Services	**3.0**	2.3
Asset Management	**3.9**	3.5
Corporate[a]	**54.2**	49.7
Total common stockholders' equity	**$118.7**	$110.7

(a) 2007 and 2006 include $41.7 billion of equity to offset goodwill and $12.5 billion and $8.0 billion, respectively, of equity, primarily related to Treasury, Private Equity and the Corporate Pension Plan.

It is these levels of economic capital that determine the performance of each business line. On page 39 of the Annual Report, JPM shows the returns by business line, which is simply computed as the ratio of net income to economic capital:

Table 4: Segment Results — Managed Basis

Segment results — Managed basis[a]
The following table summarizes the business segment results for the periods indicated.

Year ended December 31,	Total net revenue			Noninterest expense		
(in millions, except ratios)	**2007**	2006	2005	**2007**	2006	2005
Investment Bank	**$18,170**	$18,833	$15,110	**$13,074**	$12,860	$10,246
Retail Financial Services	**17,479**	14,825	14,830	**9,900**	8,927	8,585
Card Services	**15,235**	14,745	15,366	**4,914**	5,086	4,999
Commercial Banking	**4,103**	3,800	3,488	**1,958**	1,979	1,856
Treasury & Securities Services	**6,945**	6,109	5,539	**4,580**	4,266	4,050
Asset Management	**8,635**	6,787	5,664	**5,515**	4,578	3,860
Corporate	**4,245**	14	(1,133)	**1,762**	1,147	5,330
Total	**$74,812**	$65,113	$58,864	**$41,703**	$38,843	$38,926

Year ended December 31,	Net income (loss)			Return on equity		
(in millions, except ratios)	**2007**	2006	2005	**2007**	2006	2005
Investment Bank	**$3,139**	$3,674	$3,673	**15%**	18%	18%
Retail Financial Services	**3,035**	3,213	3,427	**19**	22	26
Card Services	**2,919**	3,206	1,907	**21**	23	16
Commercial Banking	**1,134**	1,010	951	**17**	18	28
Treasury & Securities Services	**1,397**	1,090	863	**47**	48	57
Asset Management	**1,966**	1,409	1,216	**51**	40	51
Corporate[b]	**1,775**	842	(3,554)	**NM**	NM	NM
Total	**$15,365**	$14,444	$8,483	**13%**	13%	8%

(a) Represents reported results on a tax-equivalent basis and excludes the impact of credit card securitizations.
(b) Net income included Income from discontinued operations of zero, $795 million and $229 million for 2007, 2006 and 2005, respectively.

3.5 RISK-BASED PERFORMANCE MEASUREMENT

RAROC calculations are used for three purposes:

1. Report past performance
2. Provide benchmarks for current products, activities and businesses
3. Guide the bank in the reallocation of its capital

The performance chart immediately suggests that given the aggregate RAROC of the JPMChase businesses of 13%, each business should be able to earn that minimum return on its economic capital. Furthermore, within a business, say card services, at a 21% RAROC, new projects and products must return at least \$0.21 per \$1.00 in incremental economic capital created.

The RAROC numbers are used to allocate capital in the future — the 51% return in asset management looks much higher than the investment bank return of 15%. Should JPM put economic capital to work in asset management at the expense of the investment bank? Perhaps, but perhaps not. The asset management group might have had a particularly good year, not expected to be repeated. The asset management business may not be able to be increased at the same level of return. Finally, the investment banking business likely adds a lot of strategic value for the JPM franchise that is not captured in the RAROC calculations.

3.6 SUMMARY

This chapter has introduced a number of key concepts and issues involved in capital management and treasury risk. Students should review this summary before proceeding.

Types of Capital

- Debt capital can best be described as capital that will be repaid, should the bank go into liquidation, after depositors and other debt holders of the bank have been repaid, but before equity capital holders.
- Equity capital constitutes fully paid ordinary shares/common stock and non-cumulative perpetual preferred shares/stock.
- The capital of a bank, subject to Basel regulation, can be described as having two major tiers: Tier 1 and Tier 2, plus one additional tier which has a very restricted use, Tier 3.
- The Basel Committee considers that the key element of capital on which supervisors should place most emphasis is equity capital, to which should be added the accrual of profits to reserves. Together these two elements constitute core capital.
- Tier 2 capital comprises debt capital that is subordinated (to the interests of depositors and other creditors) in the event of a bank going into liquidation.
- Upper Tier 2 capital is distinguished from other subordinated debt issues that pay interest (and where failure to do so would be an event of default).
- Lower Tier 2 capital comprises subordinated debt issues that pay interest. Such issues must also have a repayment date which must be at least five years on initial issue and of which only 80% of outstanding debt can count as Tier 2 capital four years before repayment, 60% in year 3, 40% in year 2, and 20% in year 1.
- Tier 3 capital is debt capital that can only be used to support market risk in the trading book of the bank.

- If the issuer has the right to repay before the scheduled repayment date (a 'call' option) the option will be ignored for capital purposes, unless the issuer is due to pay a higher rate of interest as compensation to the holder for not having exercised the option (known as a 'step up clause').

Deductions from Capital

- Goodwill can often be seen as a capital item in company balance sheets and arises as a result of the purchase of a business for more than the value of the capital of the acquired company as it is valued in that company's balance sheet.
- The balance sheet of the new (acquired plus acquiring) bank will, depending on the size of the goodwill payment made to the acquired bank's shareholders, have less Tier 1 capital than that which the banks independently had before the acquisition.
- Investments in subsidiaries engaged in banking and similar activities, where the subsidiary is not consolidated into the regulated banking group's balance sheet, will result in a deduction from capital of the book value of the equity investment.
- In a number of countries it is common for a bank to have its capital reduced by the value of the shares it holds in other banks.

Ratios Between Tiers of Capital

- The Basel Committee sets out rules for the ratios that banks should maintain between different classes of equity.
- The primary restriction is that Tier 2 capital cannot exceed 50% of a bank's total regulatory capital.

The Capital Creation Process

- The main reasons banks raise new equity capital through large share issues are as a result of:
  - The write-off of loans destroying existing capital
  - Senior management asking existing and potential shareholders to support a strategy of rapid growth in the balance sheet through either new business generation or a proposed acquisition.
- When an acquisition is being made the shareholders and markets will be more concerned with the premium to the current share price of the target bank.
- Banks which are profitable create a flow of new capital on a continuing basis, as profits after bad debt and other provisions are available for distribution to shareholders.

Economic Capital

- Economic capital is a measure of a bank's capital requirement that relates directly to the aggregate risk the bank is running.
- Value at Risk (VaR) models represented a major step forward for both management and supervisors trying to understand the risks a bank was running in its trading businesses. Clearly a bank with a higher Value at Risk (VaR) is running a higher level of risk.
- Banks have developed models that measure the potential extreme losses in scenarios that involved losses from a combination of their risks.
- Many supervisors have expressed concern that Basel II based credit grading models do not provide adequate information in the area of concentration risk management.
- The data available to 'populate' and therefore measure risk distributions of losses is difficult to assemble.
- Supervisors are often wary of accepting economic capital models as a basis for estimating regulatory capital for a combination of reasons.
- A number of sophisticated banks, however, use economic capital models to support decisions regarding the level and structure of capital that they believe they should hold.
- Under Pillar 2 of Basel II banks using such models are expected to share and discuss their results with supervisors.

RAROC (Risk Adjusted Return on Capital)

- RAROC is the return to an activity as measured by its risk rather than its cash requirements. It is well-suited for banks, where risk is more important than cash.
- RAROC is computed as the expected profit or loss of an activity net of financing costs, divided by the risk measure.
- In some cases, regulatory charges are added to the numerator of the RAROC calculation.
- In theory, RAROC should be measured on an incremental basis, but in practice, RAROC is measured for individual transactions, portfolios or bank business units.
- RAROC acts as a hurdle rate for risk-taking activities; only activities that have RAROCs exceeding a minimum threshold are accepted.

Authors

David C. Shimko, Ph.D.
Member of the Board of Trustees, Global Association of Risk Professionals

David holds a Ph.D. in Finance from Northwestern University. He has taught finance at the Kellogg Graduate School of Management at Northwestern University, the Marshall School of Business at the University of Southern California, the Harvard Business School and the Courant Institute at New York University. His professional career included managing Commodity Derivatives Research and Risk Management Research at JPMorgan, managing client Risk Management Advisory services at Bankers Trust, and co-founding Risk Capital, an independent risk advisory firm sold to Towers Perrin in 2006. As a consultant, David advised senior management in energy, banking, insurance and mining firms on all matters related to risk management policy, strategy and tactics. His publications address risk policy and governance, risk measurement and management, focusing particularly in the areas of commodities and credit. Currently, David sits on the Board of Trustees of the Global Association of Risk Professionals, and acts as an independent financial consultant to corporations and investment funds.

Peter Went, Ph.D.
Senior Researcher, GARP Research Center

Peter holds a Ph.D. in Finance from the University of Nebraska, and is a Senior Researcher at the GARP Research Center, where he develops risk management resources for GARP and conducts research in financial risk management. He taught finance at Bucknell University, University of Nebraska–Lincoln, and the Graduate School of Business at the Central European University, and worked as an investment analyst for a Nordic boutique investment firm. Currently, Peter is a member of the board of Woodlands Financial Services Corporation and a widely held technology company. His publications cover topics such as bank mergers, risks in foreign exchange and global equity markets, and banking risks. In 2009, he co-authored *Foundations of Banking Risk* published by Wiley. He holds an M.Sc in Economics from the Stockholm School of Economics, an LL.M from the Stockholm University School of Law, and is a Chartered Financial Analyst (CFA).

Footnotes

Chapter 1

1 *See www.americanbanker.com/glossary.html*

Chapter 2

1 *CFO Magazine, March 15, 2008.*

2 *See Financial Times, September 25, 1998.*

3 *Arguably, the FDIC exists partially to protect US depositors, but it also protects banks by reducing the incentives of depositors to make runs on the bank.*

4 *As we saw in Chapter 2 of Market Risk Management, a book in the GARP Series, futures margining requires a daily calculation and settlement of the trade profit or loss.*

5 *Fitch Bank Failures Study - 1990 - 2003*

6 *http://riskinstitute.ch/139350.htm*

7 *Depending on the structure of securitization transaction, the credit risk may not be fully shifted from the bank to the investors in the bonds issued by the SPV. How the regulators respond to the structure of the transaction and treat the credit risk transfer from the bank to the investors in the SPV as a result of the complex transaction is essential in understanding the potential for capital relief and liquidity improvement for the bank. Even the simplest of these approaches and transactions can be quite complex.*

8 *Financial Institution Letter FIL-84-2008, 8/28/08*

Glossary

A

Asset and Liability Management (ALM): The Asset and Liability Management (ALM) function in a bank manages the risks caused by asset and liability mismatches as well as the interest rate risk in the bank's banking book and the bank's liquidity risk.

Asset Liability Committee (ALCO): Asset Liability Committee (ALCO) is typically a committee of senior managers and board members tasked with executing and overseeing the bank's ALM activities.

B

Bank: A bank takes deposits, makes loans, arranges payments, holds a banking license and is subject to regulatory supervision by a banking regulator.

Banking book: The banking book of a bank is the portfolio of assets, primarily loans, a bank expects to hold until maturity when the loan is repaid fully; typically refers to the loans the bank underwrites.

Basel Accords: The Basel Accords (Basel I Accord, the Market Risk Amendment and the Basel II Accord) are the cornerstones of international risk-based banking regulation, the results of a collaborative attempt by banking regulators from major developed countries to create a globally valid and widely applicable framework for banks and bank risk management.

Basel Committee on Banking Supervision: The Basel Committee on Banking Supervision is a forum for regulatory cooperation between its member countries on banking supervision-related matters, was established by the central bank governors, and consists of senior representatives of bank supervisory authorities and central banks from major economies.

Basis point: A basis point is one-hundredth of one percent, or 0.0001.

Bid-ask-spread: The bid-ask-spread is the difference between the buy price or rate (bid) and sell price or rate (ask) of a financial instrument.

Board of directors: The board of directors has the ultimate responsibility for the management and performance of a company, is responsible for the bank's governance, and is elected by the shareholders.

Bond: A bond is a legally binding contract through which the borrower (also referred to as the issuer of the bond) borrows the principal, an amount specified in the bond, from an investor and in exchange pays a specified amount of interest (also referred as the coupon payment), usually at regular intervals, and at maturity repays the principal.

C

Capital adequacy: Capital adequacy is achieved when a bank's capital ratio meets or exceeds the minimum capital ratio, which under the Basel Accords is 8% of risk weighted assets and can be satisfied with Tier 1, Tier 2, and Tier 3 capital. Tier 1 capital has to account for at least 4% of risk-weighted assets; the remainder can be satisfied through Tier 2 and, in the case of market risk capital, Tier 3 capital. National banking regulators can deviate from these minimum capital adequacy ratios.

Capital requirement: Capital requirement determines how much minimum capital level regulators require each bank to hold against its risk levels.

Capital: Capital denotes financial assets or the financial value of assets, such as cash, or the long-term financial contribution of investors in a corporation.

Central bank: A central bank is the principal monetary authority of a country, or a group of countries, and may also exercise regulatory and supervisory responsibilities over other banks, arrange payment between banks, and when needed, provide stability to the financial and banking system.

Clearinghouse: A clearinghouse guarantees the financial performance of a trade on an exchange by becoming the buyer to each seller and the seller to each buyer, and provide clearing and settlement services for financial transactions.

Collateral: Collateral is an asset pledged by a borrower to secure a loan or other credit and is forfeited to the lender in the event of the borrower's default.

Commercial bank: A commercial bank offers a wide range of highly specialized loans to large businesses, acts as an intermediary in raising funds, and provides specialized financial services including payment, investment, and risk management services.

Corporate governance: Corporate governance is a set of relationships between the board of directors, shareholders and other stakeholders of an organization, outlines the relationship among these groups, sets rules how the organization should be managed, and sets its operational framework.

Cost of funds: The cost of funds is the interest rate, required return, or other compensation associated with securing and using capital.

Counterparty: Counterparty is a party to a contract who is contractually bound and is expected to perform - deliver securities, make payments, or similar - sometime in the future.

Counterparty credit risk: Counterparty credit risk is the risk that the other party to a contract or agreement will fail to perform under the terms of an agreement, and is particularly relevant for trading.

Credit risk: Credit risk is the risk of loss due to non-payment of a loan, bond, or other credit.

D

Default: Default, the failure to pay interest or principal according to contractual terms, and occurs when a debtor or a counterparty is unable to make a timely payment or delivery.

Default risk: Default risk is the potential loss due to default.

Deposit: A deposit is money entrusted to a bank for safekeeping in a bank account that allows the depositor to withdraw these funds and any interest paid by the bank on the deposit.

Derivative: A (financial) derivative does not have an intrinsic value of its own, whose value changes in response to changes in the value of a related underlying financial asset or commodity, and includes swaps, options, forwards, and futures.

Disclosure: Disclosure is the dissemination of information about the conditions of a business that allows for a proper and transparent evaluation of that business.

Dividend: A dividend is the part of the earnings of a corporation that are paid out to its owners typically either through the payment of cash or the issuance of additional shares.

Duration: Duration is a measure of price sensitivity for a fixed income instrument and quantifies the sensitivity of the price of a fixed-income investment to a small incremental change in interest rates.

E

Economic capital: Economic capital is the amount of capital the bank needs in the case of loss events, covers all risks across a bank, and is essential for the bank to survive in the long term.

Endogenous Liquidity: Endogenous liquidity is the liquidity inherent in the bank's assets themselves.

Equity: Equity is the capital raised from shareholders plus retained earnings and reflects the ownership interest in a corporation.

Equity capital: Equity capital is capital the bank has raised from shareholders and from its earnings.

Equity capital: Equity capital is capital the bank has raised from shareholders and from its earnings.

Equity risk: Equity risk is the potential loss due to an adverse change in the price of stock.

Exchange: A (financial) exchange is a formal, organized physical or electronic marketplace where trades between investors follow standardized procedures.

Exogenous liquidity: Exogenous liquidity (often called funding liquidity) is the liquidity provided to the bank by its liability structure, including its ability to borrow and obtain contingent lines.

Exposure at Default (EAD): Exposure at Default is the maximum loss the lender or counterparty may suffer in case of a default.

External liquidity: External liquidity is the noncontractual contingent capital supplied by investors and other institutions to support a bank during times of liquidity stress.

F

Fair market price: Fair market price is the price the asset would fetch if sold on the market immediately to a willing buyer.

Financial asset: A financial asset derives its value from a specific contractual claim and typically includes bonds, loans, stocks, money, currency, derivatives, certain commodities, and other assets of value.

Financial instrument: A financial instrument is a representation of an ownership interest claim or the contractual or contingent claim to receive or deliver cash, another financial instrument, or asset, and can either be a cash instrument (e.g., cash, securities, loans, bonds, notes, equity) or a derivative instrument (e.g., forward, future, option, and swap).

Fractional reserve banking: Fractional reserve banking is a banking system where only a small fraction of the total deposits must be held in reserve with the balance available to be invested in loans and other securities.

Funding liquidity risk: Funding liquidity risk refers to a bank's potential inability to have funds available to repay depositors on demand and to fund loans when needed.

Futures contract: A futures (contract), a derivative, is a standardized and transferable contract traded on an exchange that defines the delivery of specified asset (e.g., commodities, currencies, bonds or stocks), at a specified price, at a specified quantity, on a specified future date.

G

General or systematic market risk: General, or systematic, market risk is the risk of an adverse movement in the market prices that are applied across a range of financial assets, including fixed income, loans, equity, and commodities.

Goodwill: Goodwill arises as a result of the purchase of a business for more than the value of the capital of the acquired company as it is valued in that company's balance sheet. The excess payment to the shareholders of the acquired company becomes goodwill in the new consolidated balance sheet of the acquiring and acquired companies.

Governance: Governance relates to the rules, processes, policies, and regulations outlining and defining the capacity, operational management, and administration of an organization, business, or other entity.

H

Hedging: Hedging reduces risk by matching a position as closely as possible with an opposite and offsetting position in a financial instrument that tracks or mirrors the value changes in the position.

Hybrid security: A hybrid security is a financial instrument that has both equity and debt features.

I

Innovative capital: Innovative capital includes complex financial instruments that have both equity and debt features.

Insolvency: Insolvency occurs when liabilities exceed assets; while not synonymous with bankruptcy or illiquidity, it typically leads to either or both.

Interbank loan: An interbank loan is a loan between banks.

Interest rate: Interest rate, the price of credit, is the rate charged for accessing and using borrowed funds.

Interest rate risk: Interest rate risk is the potential loss of value due to the variability of interest rates.

Interest rate swap: Interest rate swap is a contractual agreement under which two parties exchange interest payments of differing nature on a predetermined amount for a known period of time with known frequency.

Interest-rate risk in the banking book: The interest rate risk in the banking book is caused by maturity differences between bank assets and liabilities, by differing interest rates used for pricing, and differering repricing points.

Internal Ratings Based (IRB) Approach: Internal Ratings Based approach to determine the regulatory minimum capital requirement for credit risk uses the bank's own information, and includes two different procedures that have methodological differences to forecast the different risk factors.

J

Junior debt: Junior debt is subordinated to more senior debt in case of bankruptcy, default or similar event, but has priority before equity.

L

Leverage: Leverage reflects the amount or proportion of debt used in the financing structure of an organization; the higher the leverage the more debt the company uses.

LIBOR (London InterBank Offered Rate): LIBOR, London Interbank Offered Rate, is a daily reference rate based on the average interest rate banks in London charge other banks, on the offer side of the transaction, when borrowing and lending.

Liquidity: Liquidity refers to either market (transactional) or funding (payment) liquidity.

Liquidity risk: Liquidity risk can be market (transactional) liquidity risk and funding (payment) liquidity risk.

Long position: A long position, the opposite of short position, represents the ownership position of an asset; when the asset's value increases, the position increases in value and when the asset's value declines, the position decreases in value.

M

Market liquidity risk: Market liquidity risk refers to conditions when trading – buying and selling – assets significantly affects their transaction price or can be only be executed at significant price concessions.

Market risk: Market risk is defined as the risk of losses in on- and off-balance-sheet positions arising from movements in market prices, and typically encompasses the risks pertaining to interest rate related instruments and equities in the trading book, and foreign exchange risk and commodities risk throughout the bank.

Mark-to-market: Marked-to-market (accounting) assigns a value to an asset that reflects the value it would fetch on the market.

Maturity: Maturity is the time period until a loan, bond or other credit is repaid fully.

N

Net interest income: Net interest income is the difference between interest income and interest expense.

Operational risk: Operational risk is the risk of loss resulting from inadequate or failed internal processes, people and systems, or from external events. This definition includes legal risk, but excludes strategic and reputational risk.

P

Paid-in-capital: Paid-in-capital is the (equity) capital that the owners have invested in the corporation.

Portfolio: A portfolio is a collection of investments, such as stocks, bonds and cash equivalents, held by an institution or a private individual.

Preferred share: A preferred share has properties of both equity and debt, and are senior to common stock, but are subordinated to bonds; usually they do not carry any voting rights.

Probabilistic model: A probabilistic model incorporates the complex and interdependent behavior of complex assets and liabilities, and incorporates statistical and quantitative modeling.

R

Rate Sensitive Assets (RSA): Rate sensitive assets are bank assets, mainly bonds, loans and leases, and the value of these assets is sensitive to changes in interest rates; these assets are either repriced or revalued as interest rates change.

Rate Sensitive Liabilities (RSL): Rate sensitive liabilities are bank liabilities, mainly interest-bearing deposits and other liabilities, and the value of these liabilities is sensitive to changes in interest rates; these liabilities are either repriced or revalued as interest rates change.

Regulatory capital requirement: Regulatory capital requirement specifies how much minimum capital a bank must hold to guard against the various – market, credit and operational – risks it takes.

Repurchase agreement or repo: A repurchase agreement, "repo", is a contract between two parties in which one party sells the other a security at a specified price with the obligation to buy the security back at a later date for another specified price; they are widely used by central banks to provide support to meet a bank's short-term liquidity.

Risk appetite: Risk appetite is the level of risk exposure an investor is willing to assume in exchange for the potential for a profit.

Risk management: Risk management is a structured approach to monitoring, measuring, and managing exposures to reduce the potential impact of an uncertain event happening.

Risk policy: A risk policy outlines the risk management framework of an organization in relationship to its objectives, and varies across and within industries and firms based on the ability to absorb losses and the rate of return they seek from operations.

Risk transfer: Risk transfer is the assumption of specific risk for a fee, or premium.

Risk-Adjusted Return on Capital (RAROC): Risk-Adjusted Return on Capital adjusts the return generated by an asset for the inherent risk assumed by the project making it easier to compare and contrast projects with different risk profiles.

Risk-weighted assets: Risk-weighted assets equal the sum of various financial assets multiplied by their respective risk-weights and off-balance sheet items weighted for their credit risk according to the regulatory requirements outlined by banking regulators and supervisors.

S

Scenario analysis: Scenario analysis, or what-if analysis, assesses the potential outcome of various scenarios by setting up several possible situations and analyzing the potential outcomes of each situation.

Securitization: Securitization is a process where illiquid cash flow producing assets (such as mortgages, credit cards, and loans, etc.) are pooled into a portfolio; the purchase of these assets in the portfolio is financed by securities issued to investors, who then share the cash flows generated by the portfolio.

Security: A (financial) security is a fungible financial instrument.

Senior bond: Senior debt has priority over all other more junior and subordinated debt in case of bankruptcy, default or similar event.

Shareholder: A shareholder, stockholder or equity holder, is one of the owners of a corporation, has the right to elect the board of directors, may decide in corporate matters, and may receive dividends.

Shareholder's equity: Shareholder's equity, the difference between assets and liabilities, is the shareholders' investment in the company, which typically equals the amount the shareholders have invested in the company and retained earnings.

Short position: A short position, the opposite of long position, represents either the selling of a borrowed asset, the writing of an option, or selling a futures position; when the asset's value increases, the position declines in value and when the asset's value declines, the position increases in value.

Solvency: Solvency denotes the financial condition of the firm when assets exceed the liabilities.

Specific, non-systematic, unique risk: Specific, non-systematic, unique risk is the risk of an adverse movement in the price of one individual security or financial asset due to factors specific to that particular security or issuer.

Speculation: Speculation involves the buying (long position), holding, selling, and short-selling (short position) of financial assets, commodities, foreign exchange, or derivatives, in the expectation that price fluctuations will generate a profit; a position that is not hedged or when simply buying or selling the asset with the hope of earning a profit.

Stakeholder: A stakeholder is someone with an interest in the future of a business, enterprise or organization, and usually includes individual customers, borrowers, depositors, investors, employees, shareholders, regulators, and public.

Standardized Approach: The Standardized Approach to calculate the bank's credit and market risk capital is the simplest approach outlined in the Basel II Accord for these risks. For operational risk, this is an intermediate level approach.

Stress testing: Stress testing assesses the potential outcome of specific changes that are fundamental, material, and adverse.

Swap: A swap, a derivative, allows two counterparties to exchange streams of future cash flows with each other.

T

Tier 1 capital: Tier 1 Capital in the Basel Accords is the core capital of the bank and refers to equity capital and to certain types of disclosed reserves as well as particular debt/equity hybrid securities. .

Tier 2 capital: Tier 2 Capital in the Basel Accords is supplementary capital and refers to undisclosed and certain disclosed reserves, general provisions, general loan loss reserves, hybrid capital instruments, and subordinated debt.

Tier 3 capital: Tier 3 Capital in the Basel Accords is a specific type of supplementary capital and refers to certain type of short-term debt that can partially satisfy regulatory minimum capital requirements for market risk only.

Trading book: The trading book of a bank is the portfolio of various positions in financial assets, instruments and commodities that a bank holds with the intention to invest, to trade, or to hedge other positions in the trading book.

Treasury risk: Treasury risk is defined as the risk of loss in the activities of a bank's Treasury.

Treasury: The treasury manages the financial aspects of an organization and in banking it typically manages the bank's asset and liability structure, liquidity, and capital exposure.

Index

A

B

C

D

E

F

G

I

L

M

N

O

P

R

S

T

Notes